T0301917

An Analysis of

Daniel Kahneman's

Thinking, Fast and Slow

Jacqueline Anne Allan

Published by Macat International Ltd
24:13 Coda Centre, 189 Munster Road, London SW6 6AW.

Distributed exclusively by Routledge
2 Park Square, Milton Park, Abingdon, Oxon OX14 4RN
711 Third Avenue, New York, NY 10017, USA

Routledge is an imprint of the Taylor & Francis Group, an informa business

www.macat.com
info@macat.com

Cataloguing in Publication Data
A catalogue record for this book is available from the British Library.

Library of Congress Cataloguing-in-Publication Data is available upon request.

Cover illustration: David Newton

ISBN 978-1-912453-99-3 (hardback)
ISBN 978-1-912453-05-4 (paperback)
ISBN 978-1-912453-20-7 (e-book)

Notice

CONTENTS

THE MACAT LIBRARY

The Macat Library is a series of unique academic explorations of seminal works in the humanities and social sciences – books and papers that have had a significant and widely recognised impact on their disciplines. It has been created to serve as much more than just a summary of what lies between the covers of a great book. It illuminates and explores the influences on, ideas of, and impact of that book. Our goal is to offer a learning resource that encourages critical thinking and fosters a better, deeper understanding of important ideas.

Each publication is divided into three Sections: Influences, Ideas, and Impact. Each Section has four Modules. These explore every important facet of the work, and the responses to it.

This Section-Module structure makes a Macat Library book easy to use, but it has another important feature. Because each Macat book is written to the same format, it is possible (and encouraged!) to cross-reference multiple Macat books along the same lines of inquiry or research. This allows the reader to open up interesting interdisciplinary pathways.

To further aid your reading, lists of glossary terms and people mentioned are included at the end of this book (these are indicated by an asterisk [*] throughout) – as well as a list of works cited.

Macat has worked with the University of Cambridge to identify the elements of critical thinking and understand the ways in which six different skills combine to enable effective thinking.
Three allow us to fully understand a problem; three more give us the tools to solve it. Together, these six skills make up the **PACIER** model of critical thinking. They are:

ANALYSIS – understanding how an argument is built
EVALUATION – exploring the strengths and weaknesses of an argument
INTERPRETATION – understanding issues of meaning

CREATIVE THINKING – coming up with new ideas and fresh connections
PROBLEM-SOLVING – producing strong solutions
REASONING – creating strong arguments

To find out more, visit **WWW.MACAT.COM.**

CRITICAL THINKING AND *THINKING, FAST AND SLOW*

Primary critical thinking skill: CREATIVE THINKING
Secondary critical thinking skill: INTERPRETATION

While it may seem antithetical to identify creative thinking as a scientist's main skill, Daniel Kahneman is not your everyday psychologist. Synthesizing ideas from a wide variety of disciplines, his unique way of looking at the world has found its way into the wider canon through *Thinking, Fast and Slow.* Kahneman puts forward the theory of a dual process model of thought, in which one process is fast and reliant on short cuts, and one is slow, deliberate, and easily fatigued. He applies this model to almost every facet of life, giving examples of the effects of faulty thinking that range from the legal system to the education system, from politics to advertising, and beyond. Although he has achieved vast insight into human error, he remains humble, explaining that he is not infallible and often makes the same mistakes. Some of his best-known theories have arisen from his own errors. It takes a truly creative mind to react to errors with curiosity rather than criticism.

Also unique to Kahneman is his interpretation of the world around him. While most are interested in emulating success, he is more interested in why we make errors. Perhaps more importantly, Kahneman has interpreted *how* we make mistakes; he gives us a framework on which to re-evaluate decisions and judgments that we have encountered and offers us insight as to why these choices were made. His creative experimental approach invites his readers to become part of his theories, to make up their own minds and to watch psychology in action within themselves. By reinterpreting human behavior, Kahneman has redefined how thought works.

Thinking, Fast and Slow is therefore a landmark work. It not only gives us an overview of Kahneman's career, during which he has received many accolades, it also gives us a bird's eye view of the whole field of psychology, and the birth of a new one – behavioral economics. In this book, Kahneman delivers his decades of knowledge to a wider general audience in the hope that we will adopt his vocabulary and think more carefully and accurately about our own thinking.

ABOUT THE AUTHOR OF THE ORIGINAL WORK

Daniel Kahneman is an Israeli psychologist born in 1934, who was educated both in Jerusalem and in the United States. He started his career in the Israeli Defense Forces, where he was tasked with assessing the suitability of candidates for officer training. His errors in these judgments and the difficulty in predicting behavior led to a life-long interest in judgment and decision-making. In 1968 he met his long-time collaborator and 'academic soul mate' Amos Tversky. Together, they would revolutionize their field, creating the foundations for an entirely new school of thought – behavioral economics. In 2002 Kahneman received the Nobel Prize for Economics for the work he did with Tversky, who sadly passed away in 1996. *Thinking, Fast and Slow* provides an overview of Kahneman's career, which has spanned multiple disciplines, from cognitive pupillometry to hedonic psychology. He was awarded the Presidential Medal of Freedom, the highest civil honor in the US, by Barack Obama in 2013.

ABOUT THE AUTHOR OF THE ANALYSIS

Jacqueline Allan is a lecturer and researcher at Birkbeck College, University of London. She holds undergraduate degrees from Kings College London and Birkbeck College.

ABOUT MACAT

GREAT WORKS FOR CRITICAL THINKING

Macat is focused on making the ideas of the world's great thinkers accessible and comprehensible to everybody, everywhere, in ways that promote the development of enhanced critical thinking skills.

It works with leading academics from the world's top universities to produce new analyses that focus on the ideas and the impact of the most influential works ever written across a wide variety of academic disciplines. Each of the works that sit at the heart of its growing library is an enduring example of great thinking. But by setting them in context – and looking at the influences that shaped their authors, as well as the responses they provoked – Macat encourages readers to look at these classics and game-changers with fresh eyes. Readers learn to think, engage and challenge their ideas, rather than simply accepting them.

'Macat offers an amazing first-of-its-kind tool for interdisciplinary learning and research. Its focus on works that transformed their disciplines and its rigorous approach, drawing on the world's leading experts and educational institutions, opens up a world-class education to anyone.'

Andreas Schleicher
Director for Education and Skills, Organisation for Economic
Co-operation and Development

'Macat is taking on some of the major challenges in university education … They have drawn together a strong team of active academics who are producing teaching materials that are novel in the breadth of their approach.'

Prof Lord Broers,
former Vice-Chancellor of the University of Cambridge

'The Macat vision is exceptionally exciting. It focuses upon new modes of learning which analyse and explain seminal texts which have profoundly influenced world thinking and so social and economic development. It promotes the kind of critical thinking which is essential for any society and economy.
This is the learning of the future.'

Rt Hon Charles Clarke, former UK Secretary of State for Education

'The Macat analyses provide immediate access to the critical conversation surrounding the books that have shaped their respective discipline, which will make them an invaluable resource to all of those, students and teachers, working in the field.'

Professor William Tronzo, University of California at San Diego

WAYS IN TO THE TEXT

KEY POINTS

- Daniel Kahneman is an Israeli psychologist who was awarded the Nobel Prize* for Economics in 2002.

- *Thinking, Fast and Slow* is primarily focused on explaining models of human judgment and decision-making.

- The book represents the culmination of a lifetime of work undertaken by the author and his collaborators. It argues that humans have two types of thought process: one fast, easy, and prone to error, and one slow, difficult and more accurate and analytical.

Who Is Daniel Kahneman?

Daniel Kahneman is an Israeli-born psychologist who researches human judgment and decision-making. He was a child in Paris at the start of World War II* and lived through the Holocaust.* His career spans over six decades, and started in the Israeli Defense Forces.*

Kahneman has worked at many prestigious universities, and is currently Professor Emeritus* at Princeton and a fellow of the Center for Rationality at the Hebrew University in Jerusalem. *Thinking, Fast and Slow* was released in 2011 for a popular audience, but Kahneman is perhaps most recognized for his 2002 Nobel Prize win. He was awarded the Memorial Prize in Economic Sciences for the work which he undertook with his long-time collaborator Amos Tversky,* who passed away in 1996. This work was also the foundation on which was built the new discipline of behavioral economics*, the study of how psychology affects economic decision-making.

Kahneman and Tversky challenged the prevailing theory of the time, that people are "rational actors" and always make decisions logically. More recently he turned his hand to hedonic psychology,* or the psychology of happiness, where he has also had a large impact. Aside from the 2002 Nobel, Kahneman has won many awards, including the Lifetime Contribution Award of the American Psychological Association,* and the Presidential Medal of Freedom.* He has been called the world's most influential living psychologist.[1]

What Does *Thinking, Fast and Slow* Say?

Thinking, Fast and Slow tells us that there are two routes people use to think. The idea of two systems of cognition* is known as a dual processing theory.* These two types of cognition are known as System 1, or the intuitive system, and System 2, or the deliberate system. These two routes, while conceptual, represent very different ways of processing information from the world around us. System 1 is always active and waiting to jump into operation. This is the system that tells us to run from danger, or gets an intuitive sense of someone's personality within seconds of meeting them. System 1 is reliant on mental operations, such as heuristics* (mental shortcuts) and biases* (leanings towards or against something based on associative memory*). This is the fast thinking of the book's title. System 2 is slow thinking. This system needs deliberate activation. It requires attention and effort and as such is not sustainable for long periods of time; it is susceptible to burnout. We use System 2 to calculate a complex equation or to answer an exam question.

It seems we should make decisions with our rational, logical System 2 all of the time, but System 2 tires easily and so we are far more reliant on System 1 than we would like to believe. Often this is no bad thing. System 1 learns from experience and can make correct intuitive judgments in situations where we lack information. In certain careers, such as law enforcement or the military, System 1 decisions can make the difference between life and death. However, System 1 is limited as it is reliant on shortcuts and is therefore prone to error.

Although Kahneman won the Nobel Prize for applying these theories to economics, thus creating the entirely new discipline of behavioral economics, he is interested in far more than just financial decision-making. He talks about System 1 errors in relation to many aspects of human experience, including happiness, politics, education, marketing, and the legal system. For instance, he asked participants in one experiment to rate whether they think that people are happier in California than in other places, and the majority said yes. Kahneman explains that when thinking about California, participants focused on one aspect that differentiates it from most other places, its hot weather, and made an assumption that the weather must make people happier without taking anything else into consideration. He calls this "the focusing illusion." *Thinking, Fast and Slow* is full of examples that demonstrate how reliance on System 1 shortcuts leads to faulty thinking.

Why Does *Thinking, Fast and Slow* Matter?

The ideas in *Thinking, Fast and Slow* are applicable to a whole spectrum of human thought, action, and behavior. It contains lessons whether the reader is looking at buying a house or examining potential biases they may have towards people. Kahneman gives us the terminology to describe the errors that we commonly make. He also gives us wider insights into society and the catastrophic effects that such errors can have, such as the tendency for judges to hand out stiffer sentences before lunch than after. Kahneman puts this particular pattern down to System 2 giving up under the strain of hunger, and the decision-making involved in passing judgment being carried out by System 1, which is reliant on shortcuts and therefore more liable to be harsh. *Thinking, Fast and Slow* highlights that even professions we associate with high levels of System 2 functioning, such as academia or law, are vulnerable to System 1 errors.

It is important to note that Kahneman also disseminates the work of others in *Thinking, Fast and Slow*, giving the reader an opportunity to learn about the evolution of its main themes. In this sense it is more than just a digestible overview of Kahneman's work; it is also a compendium of relevant thought. After publication some of the studies that were used as examples in the book came under closer scrutiny and it was found that the results could not be replicated (replication is a hallmark of sound research). This forced many in the field to take another look at the validity of established claims. Kahneman was one of the leaders of this movement for more rigorous research practices.

NOTES

1   "Daniel Kahneman Changed the Way We Think About Thinking. But What Do Other Thinkers Think of Him," *Guardian*, February 16, 2014, accessed September 14, 2017, https://www.theguardian.com/science/2014/feb/16/daniel-kahneman-thinking-fast-and-slow-tributes.

SECTION 1
INFLUENCES

MODULE 1
THE AUTHOR AND THE HISTORICAL CONTEXT

KEY POINTS

- Daniel Kahneman is a Nobel Prize winner in Economics.

- He is Jewish and was born in Tel Aviv, but he was living in Paris when World War II broke out.

- As a young scientist living in a newly formed country and working in a young discipline, he was afforded many academic freedoms.

Why Read This Text?

It is rare that a Nobel Prize winner writes an accessible popular science book. *Thinking, Fast and Slow* is a compilation of Kahneman's life's work and a comprehensive explanation of other research important to the field of behavioral economics. Kahneman's style in the book, just as in his experiments, is to constantly ask the reader "What do you think?" or "What was the first thing that came into your mind?" In this way, not only is the reader learning, they become an active participant in the experiments, make the same errors, and this in turn challenges them to reflect on their own thinking.

Although this book acts as a compendium of many people's work on behavioral economics, Kahneman's theories on thinking are more relevant than ever. He illustrates how faulty thinking affects nearly all factors of public and private life, from advertising to education, from criminal justice to stereotyping strangers. *Thinking, Fast and Slow* is essential reading for anyone who is interested in human behavior. Given that we live in a climate where we are constantly being asked to think about privilege, subconscious bias, racism, sexism, negative

> ❝ I was terrified (he) would notice the star inside my sweater. He was speaking to me with great emotion, in German. When he put me down, he opened his wallet, showed me a picture of a boy, and gave me some money. I went home more certain than ever that my mother was right: people were endlessly complicated and interesting. ❞
>
> Daniel Kahneman, *Thinking, Fast and Slow*

stereotyping, etc., *Thinking, Fast and Slow* illuminates why examining our own ways of thinking and checking for errors is so important.

Author's Life

Daniel Kahneman was born in Tel Aviv, Israel in 1934. His parents were Lithuanian Jews who ordinarily lived in Paris, having emigrated there in the early 1920s. They became reasonably successful and his father was employed as head of research in a chemical plant. This early stability was shattered by the outbreak of World War II. During the war Kahneman's father was interned for a time at Drancy, France, which was an intermediate stop between arrest and the concentration camps. His employers intervened and assured his release, making him one of the lucky few to survive. Kahneman's family fled to various locations in France, until his father died of untreated diabetes in 1944. Following D-Day,* Kahneman and his remaining family were granted permits to relocate to Palestine.

At the age of 17, when all Jewish citizens were expected to participate in military service, Kahneman decided to pursue a placement that would also allow him to complete a degree at the Hebrew University in Jerusalem. Majoring in Psychology and minoring in Mathematics, he completed his studies while working in officer training over the summer holidays.[1] This early experience had a profound effect on Kahneman and frequently exposed him to failure, particularly in predicting officer performance. He later said that the problems he grappled with "at that time were the seed of the paper on the psychology of intuitive prediction that Amos Tversky and I published much later."[2]

On being released from service in 1956, Kahneman was granted a PhD fellowship at the University of California, Berkeley. In 1961 he returned to the Psychology department at Hebrew University, where he worked until he moved to the University of British Columbia in 1978. He also taught briefly at Michigan, Cambridge and Harvard. His current role is Professor Emeritus of Psychology at Princeton University.

Over his career he has received many awards, the most prestigious being the Nobel Prize for Economics, which he won in 2002. More recently, he was awarded the Presidential Medal of Freedom by Barack Obama* in 2013.

Kahneman was 77 years old when *Thinking, Fast and Slow* was first published in October 2011.

Author's Background

His early years spent under Nazi occupation make it understandable that Kahneman would be so interested in how people think and why they make the errors they do. It is no coincidence that his first professional positions involved measuring and assessing human behavior, predicting how they would act in given situations. He also appears to have been blessed with significant freedom in terms of designing experiments and programs. It is important to note that Kahneman entered an emerging field in a brand-new country—Israel. Regarding his psychological career, he states that while it might seem odd that such a young officer would be given responsibility for setting up the interview system for an entire army, "one should remember that the state of Israel and its institutions were only seven years old at the time. That improvisation was the norm and that professionalism did not exist."[3]

Kahneman was free to run whatever experimental procedures or assessments he felt necessary to aid in his job, something that today would be unthinkable. There is a positivity bias in psychological research which favors correct hypotheses and failure is not something that is encouraged, but Kahneman's circumstances meant that he was not constrained by this. He often failed and made errors, and he saw these mistakes as an interesting feature of his work, not something to be ignored. It was on these failures and errors that Kahneman eventually built his career. In that sense he is a researcher of his time and it is difficult to imagine another period when he would have been afforded such leeway to examine failures.

NOTES

1 Daniel Kahneman, "Biographical," Nobelprize.org, accessed August 21, 2016, https://www.nobelprize.org/nobel_prizes/economic-sciences/laureates/2002/kahneman-bio.html.

2 Daniel Kahneman, "Biographical."

3 Daniel Kahneman, "Biographical."

MODULE 2
ACADEMIC CONTEXT

KEY POINTS

- Following the horrors of World War II, psychologists were asking themselves how such acts could have been committed.
- In the field of judgment and decision-making the prevailing view was that people were "rational actors."
- Kahneman revolutionized the field with his work, often carried out in partnership with Amos Tversky.

The Work in its Context

In the 1950s Solomon Asch* undertook a number of experiments that involved asking participants to judge how long a line was in relation to other lines. Under many experimental conditions participants were put in a group in which a confederate* would state the obviously incorrect answer. Asch found that rather than sticking with their own view, which was correct, participants would sometimes change their answers to conform.[1] Stanley Milgram* would extend these results by conducting what is perhaps the best-known experiment in psychological history. Following the Nuremburg Trials,* psychologists were shocked by defendants who stated that they were just following orders. Many exclaimed that this could never happen in America. Stanley Milgram tested this assumption by conducting a series of experiments whereby American participants recruited via a local newspaper (and thus bucking the trend of exclusively using undergraduate students) were asked by an authority figure to shock another participant (actually a confederate) to aid them in learning. The confederate would feign agony, but the shocks,

> ❝ Social Scientists in the 1970s broadly accepted two ideas about human nature. First, people are generally rational, and their thinking is normally sound. Second, emotions such as fear, affection, and hatred explain most of the occasions on which people depart from rationality. ❞
>
> Daniel Kahneman, *Thinking, Fast and Slow*

unbeknownst to those under study, were not real. The participant was faced with increasing voltage that went from "Slight Shock" to "Danger: Severe Shock" to "XXX."[2] When polled, staff and students at Yale University predicted that nearly no American participant would obey when asked to increase the voltage to "XXX level,[3] but the experiments showed that in the initial condition 65% did. This was a major upset to many academics. At this point in history, psychologists were coming to realize that people often behave in ways opposed to their predictions. Interestingly, those involved in the experiments later reported being somewhat dumbfounded at their actions (saying the wrong line length in Asch's experiment or shocking their peers in Milgram's), and admitted to acting in a way they, and researchers, would not consider rational.

Overview of the Field

Before Kahneman's work, particularly that which he under took with Amos Tversky, and which is described at length in *Thinking, Fast and Slow*, theorists believed that when faced with judgments and decisions, people would behave rationally. This was known as the rational agent* theory. This view from the neoclassical school* of the 1860s was predominant not only among economists but also among all manner of other theorists, including those in social and behavioral science. This, combined with emergent technology, provided a new analogy from which to describe brain activity: the mind as a computer. It was assumed that, like computers, people synthesized information and then made a summative judgment based on logic. Where judgment and decision-making violated these assumptions it was argued to be due to emotional interruption; fear, anger, hatred and affection may add a bug to the code, to extend the computer analogy.

Although Kahneman's work in this field was ground-breaking, already in the 1950s the social scientist Herbert Simon* was proposing the idea that there were boundaries to the rational agent model and coined the term "heuristic," on which Kahneman has based much of his work, to describe a mental shortcut that decision-makers use to deal with such limitations. Simon concluded that although shortcuts are used, people are still rational overall. He called this theory "bounded rationality."[4]

Academic Influences

Kahneman lists too many of his influences in *Thinking, Fast and Slow* to mention them all here. His most important and well-known influence was his academic partner of many years, Amos Tversky, of whom he says that "Amos was often described by people who knew him as the smartest person they knew."[5] The pair had similar backgrounds, both serving in the Israeli armed forces and being educated in Israel and the United States. They became friends in 1968, when Kahneman invited Tversky to give a guest lecture to his students at the Hebrew University. While he praised Tversky for the quality of his presentation, he also let him know that he completely disagreed with his theoretical position. This sparked a conversation that led to them agreeing to collaborate. Kahneman talks fondly about their blossoming academic partnership, saying "The experience was magical. I had enjoyed collaborative work before, but this was something different."[6] In 1971 they published their first joint work, *Belief in the Law of Small Numbers*,[7] and they collaborated up until Tversky's death from melanoma in 1996. It was for work undertaken alongside Tversky that Kahneman was awarded the Nobel Prize. *Thinking, Fast and Slow* opens in memory of Kahneman's long time collaborator and friend.

NOTES

1 Solomon E. Asch and H Guetzkow, "Effects of group pressure upon the modification and distortion of judgments," *Groups, Leadership, and Men* (1951): 222-236.

2 Stanley Milgram, *Obedience to Authority; An Experimental View* (New York: HarperCollins,1974).

3 Stanley Milgram, "Behavioral Study of Obedience." *The Journal of Abnormal and Social Psychology* 67, no. 4 (1963): 371.

4 Herbert Simon, "A Behavioral Model of Rational Choice", in *Models of Man, Social and Rational: Mathematical Essays on Rational Human Behavior in a Social Setting* (New York: Wiley, 1957).

5 Daniel Kahneman, "Biographical," Nobelprize.org, accessed August 21, 2016, https://www.nobelprize.org/nobel_prizes/economic-sciences/laureates/2002/kahneman-bio.html.

6 Kahneman, "Biographical."

7 Amos Tversky, and Daniel Kahneman. "Belief in the law of small numbers." *Psychological Bulletin* 76, no. 2 (1971): 105.

MODULE 3
THE PROBLEM

KEY POINTS

- Kahneman suggests alternative models to the rational agent theory for how we make judgments and decisions and why they are so often wrong.
- Kahneman believes in working with his detractors in "adversarial collaborations."*
- Kahneman is considered one of the founding fathers of behavioral economics.

Core Question

Thinking, Fast and Slow is mostly concerned with how and why humans make judgments and decisions and perhaps more importantly why we make so many errors. Kahneman's work was in opposition to the prevailing idea that people are rational agents who, when faced with making judgments and decisions, will think logically and statistically. Using many different experimental protocols Kahneman proved that the picture was far more complicated. In *Thinking, Fast and Slow* he describes, among others, two newer theories. The first he called "The law of least effort."* He ascertains that System 2 is lazy, has a limited capacity and is reliant on many facets of System 1 to operate. Essentially, we perform the operations that are easiest and require the least effort, but when we use such shortcuts, errors can occur. The second theory he calls "What you see is all there is"* or WYSIATI for short. This rule explains that we make up the best story we can to fit what data we have available. Very often there is missing information and our story is wrong, but due to overconfidence we are convinced that what we tell ourselves is true or correct. An example of this is

> ❝ The world makes much less sense than you think. The coherence comes mostly from the way your mind works. ❞
>
> Daniel Kahneman, *Thinking, Fast and Slow*

judging someone immediately or getting a "first impression." You have very limited information about the person in front of you, yet you still feel confident in your judgment of that person's character.

The Participants

Kahneman works on so many facets of decision-making and judgment theory that he has inevitably acquired detractors. What is unique about him as an academic is his attitude to criticism. He likes to engage in "adversarial collaborations," asking scholars who disagree with him to undertake joint research.

He used this strategy to ease his tense relationship with Gary Klein,* the head of another school of thought known as Naturalistic Decision Making* (NMD). NMD is concerned with how intuition appears in naturalistic settings, mostly among experts (Klein started with firefighters) and can't be replicated in a lab. It attempts to answer questions of how, in challenging environments where information is scarce, we are still able to make intuitive decisions, and contradicts Kahneman's shortcuts and experimental approach. Kahneman invited Klein to collaborate to see if there were boundaries to each other's theories and although they never fully agreed they did, over the space of 8 or 9 years, become friends. The record of their collaboration, titled "Conditions for Intuitive Expertise: A Failure to Disagree,"[1] was published in 2009. It describes "the authors' attempt to map the boundary conditions that separate true intuitive skill from overconfident and biased impressions,"[2] representing a combination of theoretical leanings.

Not all of Kahneman's detractors have been so accommodating. German psychologist Gerd Gigerenzer* has criticized *Thinking, Fast and Slow* for taking a negative view of human thought. He argues that "in concentrating only on fallacies and biases Danny pushes the idea that people are dumb,"[3] and says that with a little education on risk most people would make better decisions. He also proposes that people's decisions are right more often than Kahneman suggests. Similarly to Klein, Gigerenzer argues that decision-making cannot be formulated and is therefore unpredictable, and advocates against using probabilities as absolutes.

The Contemporary Debate

Many have credited Daniel Kahneman and Amos Tversky as the founding fathers of behavioral economics. Emerging in the late '70s, behavioral economics represents a bridge between cognitive psychology* and economics. It explains how psychological, social, and emotional factors affect financial decision-making. Kahneman and Tversky's most important contributions to the field involved explaining how people tend to be risk-averse and how framing decisions can have a huge impact. An example of this given in *Thinking, Fast and Slow* is that people would prefer to have a medical procedure with an 80% chance of survival than a 20% chance of death, even though these are exactly the same thing. Prospect theory,*[4] for which the duo were partly awarded the Nobel Prize for Economics, explains how people make decisions based on perceived gains rather than potential losses.

These theories have spawned many followers. Notable mentions include Stephen Dubner* and Stephen Levitt,* the authors of *Freakonomics*,[5] which explains unusual economic phenomena in alternative ways; Michael Lewis,* who has written about striking economic events such as the 2008 financial crash,* and has also published a book about the relationship between Kahneman and

Tversky; Malcom Gladwell,* who writes about psychological
concepts such as intuition for a popular audience; Richard Thaler*
and Cass Sunstein,* authors of *Nudge*;[6] and Nassim Taleb,* who has
influenced Kahneman considerably, particularly with his work *The
Black Swan*,[7] which details the psychology surrounding unforeseeable
events (such as 9/11*) and is explicitly mentioned throughout
Thinking, Fast and Slow.

NOTES

1   Daniel Kahneman and Gary Klein, "Conditions for Intuitive Expertise: A
    Failure to Disagree," *American Psychologist* 64:6 (2009): 515.

2   Kahneman and Klein, "Conditions for Intuitive Expertise."

3   Tim Adams "Nudge Economics: Has push come to shove for a fashionable
    theory?" *The Guardian* 1 June 2014, accessed 19 October 2017,
    https://www.theguardian.com/science/2014/jun/01/nudge-economics-
    freakonomics-daniel-kahneman-debunked.

4   Daniel Kahneman and Amos Tversky, "Prospect Theory: An analysis of
    decision under risk," *Econometrica: Journal of the Econometric Society*
    (1979): 263-291.

5   Stephen J. Dubner and Steven D. Levitt, *Freakonomics* (Ediciones B, 2014).

6   Richard Thaler and Cass Sunstein, *Nudge: The Gentle Power of Choice
    Architecture* (New Haven: Yale, 2008).

7   Nassim NicholasTaleb, *The Black Swan: The Impact of the Highly Improbable*
    (New York: Random House, 2007).

MODULE 4
THE AUTHOR'S CONTRIBUTION

KEY POINTS

- Kahneman hopes that by reading *Thinking, Fast and Slow* people will pick up vocabulary to use in their everyday lives.
- He gives both experimental and everyday examples of his theories in action.
- He was influenced by a number of different schools, which is what makes his work so original.

Author's Aims

One of the things about *Thinking, Fast and Slow* that sets it apart from other works of popular psychology is Kahneman's statement that his "goal is to introduce a language for thinking and talking about the mind."[1] In this sense, he is trying to normalize and explain complicated psychological phenomena for the general public. In order to do this he gives us the benefit of his more than fifty years in experimental psychology and behavioral economics. He wants to challenge us to think about our own thinking and more importantly to pay more attention to how we make judgments and decisions. Kahneman wants us to question our own biases and errors, our faulty System 1 operations. He also wants us to be able to realize when something or someone is trying to manipulate us, in the knowledge that as humans we rely on these shortcuts. For example, in *Thinking, Fast and Slow* Kahneman talks about how we may vote for leaders based on their looks. Square jaws suggest dominance and strength and therefore we may be more likely to vote using that criterion than really looking into the candidate's attributes. He remains humble, however, explaining that even though he is telling us these things he still makes the same mistakes as everyone else.

❝ Every author, I suppose, has in mind a setting in which readers of his or her work could benefit from having read it. Mine is the proverbial office water-cooler, where opinions are shared and gossip is exchanged. I hope to enrich the vocabulary that people use when they talk about the judgments and choices of others. ❞

Daniel Kahneman, *Thinking, Fast and Slow*

Approach

Although Kahneman is known as one of the founding fathers of behavioral economics, it becomes obvious while reading *Thinking, Fast and Slow* that he is at heart an experimental psychologist. Many of the experiments that Kahneman has undertaken and those of many of his influences, collaborators, and contemporaries are reported and explained in this book. In this sense *Thinking, Fast and Slow* is not just a record of Kahneman's work, but an overview of the entire field.

By reporting these experiments Kahneman seeks to show that people rely on biases, heuristics etc. (essentially System 1 short cuts) when making decisions, and that System 2 has a limited capacity. His traditional approach has been to find an error or an illogical process, reproduce it under experimental conditions, and explain it. On top of reporting the experiments that he and others have been involved in, Kahneman also gives everyday examples. One such is asking a friend to complete a complex math problem while walking, which results in the person having to stop while doing the calculation mentally. Kahneman was one of the first scientists to suggest that there is equivalency between cognitive and physical effort. This is why your friend stops—he is struggling to do two effortful things at once. By giving these examples Kahneman is not only demonstrating his theories, he is asking the reader to be an active participant in proving them.

Contribution in Context

Kahneman has integrated lessons learnt early in his career into the theories represented in *Thinking, Fast and Slow.* One of his earliest influences was Paul Meehl,* author of *Clinical versus Statistical Prediction.*[2] Kahneman said of this work, "It certainly had a big effect on me."[3] He used its recommendations to improve his ability to predict officer performance in the Israeli Defense Forces. He realized that there were ways to measure aspects of judgment and decision-making, an understanding which later went on to influence his experimental approach.

During his studies at Hebrew University, Kahneman was exposed to various disciplines and academics, including the social psychologist Kurt Lewin,* who profoundly influenced him. As he states, "Fifty years later, I still draw on Lewin's analysis of how to induce changes in behavior."[4] This influence can be seen in the way that Kahneman asks us to constantly evaluate our decisions, to understand if we need to change.

Also while at Hebrew University, the young Kahneman attended weekly lectures by Yeshayahu Leibowitz,* a renowned polymath who lectured in biochemistry, organic chemistry and neurophysiology. Kahneman reported that once he attended a lecture even though the temperature was 41 degrees Celsius (106 degrees Fahrenheit), saying "they were simply not to be missed."[5] Kahneman's career went on to mirror that of Leibowitz somewhat. He is unafraid to cross disciplinary boundaries and welcomes input from other schools of thought. Perhaps because of this he went on to study under David Rapaport* who believed that hidden inside Freud's* *Interpretation of Dreams** was a theory of memory and thought, based around cathexis (mental energy). Kahneman later said of this period in his life that it laid the foundations for his book *Attention and Effort.*[6]

Kahneman has had such an enormous effect on psychology because he takes ideas from a multitude of disciplines and synthesizes them into his own theories.

NOTES

1   Daniel Kahneman, *Thinking, Fast and Slow*, (London: Penguin, 2012), 13.

2   Paul E. Meehl, *Clinical Versus Statistical Prediction: A Theoretical Analysis and a Review of the Evidence* (Minneapolis: University of Minnesota Press, 1954).

3   Daniel Kahneman, "Biographical," Nobelprize.org, accessed August 21, 2016, https://www.nobelprize.org/nobel_prizes/economic-sciences/laureates/2002/kahneman-bio.html.

4   Kahneman, "Biographical."

5   Kahneman, "Biographical."

6   Daniel Kahneman, *Attention and Effort*, (NJ: Prentice-Hall, 1973).

SECTION 2
IDEAS

MODULE 5
MAIN IDEAS

KEY POINTS

- Kahneman is primarily interested in how people make judgments and decisions.

- *Thinking, Fast and Slow* explains that there are two systems of thought. The first is fast, automatic and relies on shortcuts. The second is conscious, logical and tires easily.

- *Thinking, Fast and Slow* was written for a popular audience and as such is accessible in terms of writing style.

Key Themes

In the introduction to *Thinking, Fast and Slow,* Kahneman explains that the book is divided into five parts. Part 1 is concerned with explaining his idea that thinking happens via two different routes. System 1 is the fast route and it is largely influenced by associative memory.* It is engaged subconsciously, whereas System 2 is deliberately, consciously operated. Kahneman also calls these the intuitive and the deliberate system. In part 2 he focuses on the limitations of System 1 in relation to statistical thinking, and asks the question "why is it so difficult for us to think statistically."[1] Part 3 explores why decision-making is so influenced by overconfidence and incorrect assumptions we make about our minds. It discusses solutions we use to make decisions and judgments while uncertain, and why we are so often wrong. In part 4 Kahneman explores the theory he helped discredit, that of the rational agent as proposed by early economists. He brings in the idea of the two-system theory and combines it with his earlier work with Amos Tversky on prospect theory. He explains how flaws in System 1, such

> ❝ I describe mental life by the metaphor of two agents, called System 1 and System 2, which respectively produce fast and slow thinking. I speak of the features of intuitive and deliberate thought as if they were traits and dispositions of two characters in your mind. ❞
>
> Daniel Kahneman, *Thinking, Fast and Slow*

as the vulnerability to framing effects,* are in direct contradiction to the notion that we are rational decision makers. Part 5 describes Kahneman's work on hedonic psychology* (the psychology of happiness). He updates his previous work with recent research and proposes a further two-system model of two selves, the remembering self* and the experiencing self,* "which do not have the same interests."[2] He combines this with the theory of Systems 1 and 2 by stating that if we understand the rules governing these systems, we can effectively change our experience of memory.

Exploring the Ideas

The main idea of *Thinking, Fast and Slow* is that human cognition is divided between two differing systems. System 1 is instinctual, intuitive, and fast; in it thinking occurs automatically and without any processing. System 1 is always running, ready to jump into action. In contrast, System 2 requires conscious effort and is slower. This type of thinking can't be sustained over a long period of time. Kahneman explains that "Although System 2 believes itself to be where the action is, the automatic System 1 is the hero of the book."[3] However, as System 1 is the quickest, we rely on it too much, and it in turn is reliant on shortcuts. While we may like to believe that we are governed by System 2, with our logical brains dictating our actions and behaviors, in fact we are often governed by the automatic, subconscious responses sent from System 1. As Kahneman states, "I describe

System 1 as effortlessly originating impressions and feelings that are the main source of the explicit beliefs and deliberate choices of System 2."[4]

In demonstrating some of the capabilities of System 1 he gives examples, including detecting that one object is more distant than another, detecting hostility in a voice, and recognizing that a "meek and tidy soul with a passion for detail" resembles an occupational stereotype.[5] He opposes these with examples of System 2 operations, such as comparing two washing machines for overall value, or checking the validity of a complex logical argument.[6]

Kahneman is eager to point out that most thought constitutes an interaction between the systems. If there is something in the environment that is contradictory to what System 1 expects, then System 2 is engaged. Kahneman explains that "The division of labor between System 1 and System 2 is highly efficient: it minimizes effort and optimizes performance."[7]

Language and Expression

Although Kahneman is an academic, *Thinking, Fast and Slow* has been praised by both academics and journalists for being accessible to all. Writing for the global news website *The Daily Beast*, journalists Malcolm Jones and Lucas Wittman state that the book is for "anyone interested in economics, cognitive science, and, in short, human behavior,"[8] while Jacek Debiec calls it "detailed, yet accessible" in the scientific journal *Nature*.[9] Kahneman has a history of connecting with his audience. Speaking of his early work successes, he states "We almost always included in our articles the full text of the questions we had asked ourselves and our respondents,"[10] allowing readers to take part mentally in the experiments and notice their own thinking errors.

Thinking, Fast and Slow follows suit, and is full of such examples. Bringing the academic theories to a larger popular audience is what Kahneman wanted to achieve. He wanted to bring a larger vocabulary to the conversations not just of economists and academics but to "the proverbial water cooler." He wants all of us to think about our decision-making and our intuitions more carefully. It is also for this reason that he provides examples of how we may use the language he does, in everyday conversation in his "Speaking of…" section at the end of each chapter. For example, at the end of chapter 1 he suggests that one might say in conversation "This was a pure System 1 response. She reacted to the threat before she recognized it."[11]

When thinking about expression of the ideas in *Thinking, Fast and Slow*, it is important to note that when we speak of System 1 and System 2 we are talking conceptually, not concretely. Kahneman explains that "System 1 and System 2 are so central to the story I tell in this book that I must make it absolutely clear that they are fictitious characters."[12] This at first may seem confusing but Kahneman is trying to explain that these systems are not physiologically visible; you won't find them as areas in the brain. Kahneman counters any challenges to this way of presenting his ideas by saying "that the characters are useful because of some quirks of our minds, yours and mine."[13]

NOTES

1   Daniel Kahneman, *Thinking, Fast and Slow*, (London: Penguin, 2012), 13.

2   *Thinking, Fast and Slow*, 14.

3   *Thinking, Fast and Slow*, 21.

4   *Thinking, Fast and Slow*, 21.

5   *Thinking, Fast and Slow*, 21.

6   *Thinking, Fast and Slow*, 23.

7   *Thinking, Fast and Slow*, 24 – 25.

8   Malcom Jones and Lucas Wittman, "Fall Books Preview: From Murakami to Joan Didion," *The Daily Beast*, February 9, 2011, accessed August 21, 2017, http://www.thedailybeast.com/fall-books-preview-from-murakami-to-

joan-didion.

9   Jacek Debiec, "Neuroscience: Capturing free will." *Nature* 478, no. 7369
    (2011): 322-323.

10 *Thinking, Fast and Slow*, 9.

11 *Thinking, Fast and Slow*, 30.

12 *Thinking, Fast and Slow*, 29.

13 *Thinking, Fast and Slow*, 29.

MODULE 6
SECONDARY IDEAS

KEY POINTS

- Kahneman states that we rely on shortcuts in the form of heuristics, biases, effects,* illusions,* and fallacies* in order to make judgments and decisions.

- Mental effort can be viewed on a spectrum from cognitive ease* to cognitive strain,* and ease is the most pleasurable state.

- Some of Kahneman's ideas may be difficult for people to accept as they challenge personal beliefs about the self.

Other Ideas

One of the main themes that runs through *Thinking, Fast and Slow* is that we use cognitive shortcuts in order to make judgments and decisions. Kahneman calls these shortcuts biases, effects, illusions, fallacies, and heuristics.

A heuristic is what Kahneman calls "a rule of thumb." For instance, he describes the affect heuristic,* which explains that people "let their likes and dislikes determine their beliefs about in the world."[1] For example, "Your political preference determines the arguments you find compelling."[2]

A bias is a tendency towards something due to prior knowledge. Confirmation bias* describes how we are quicker to believe something that fits with knowledge we already have. For example, if you have a bias against immigrants then you will pay more attention to negative news reports about that group or even actively seek information that confirms your original assertion.

❝ For some of our most important beliefs we have no evidence at all, except that people we love and trust hold these beliefs. Considering how little we know, the confidence we have in our beliefs is preposterous – and it is also essential. ❞

Daniel Kahneman, *Thinking, Fast and Slow*

An effect can broadly be described as a subconscious psychological phenomenon. In *Thinking, Fast and Slow* Kahneman covers many of these. One is the mere exposure effect,* in which simply exposing someone to something makes them more likely to favor it. Another is the halo effect,* whereby we are likely to judge the actions of someone we like as correct and make excuses for mistakes.

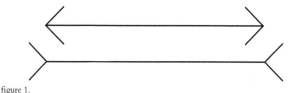

figure 1.

An illusion is an impression of something that is not correct. This can either be visual, as in the case of the Muller-Lyer illusion,*[3] whereby two lines of equal length appear to be different (see figure 1), or cognitive, that is an illusion of thought. An example of a cognitive illusion is the illusion of skill,* whereby we judge a person skilled when they have success in an activity, when actually the results of those decisions were down to luck and not expertise.

A fallacy is a falsehood that we tell ourselves, usually arising from overconfidence. For example, in the planning fallacy,* a group undertaking a forecasting task will only take into consideration their current situation and not that of others who have had similar tasks in the past, thus ignoring valuable information. If they had looked at base rates of success for similar endeavors, they would not have made wildly optimistic judgments while planning.

Exploring the Ideas

In relation to the broader theme of *Thinking, Fast and Slow* these shortcuts represent System 1 operations. Using biases, heuristics, effects, fallacies, and illusions is how we think "fast." We like to think that our logical mind, System 2, is in control, but we have to work hard to ensure that we check our judgments and decisions for errors due to over-reliance on System 1 shortcuts. To explain why we rely on these shortcuts, Kahneman writes that when thinking about mental effort we should envisage a cockpit, where "One of the dials measures *cognitive ease* and its range is between "Easy" and "Strained.""[4] For Kahneman, the easy position suggests that everything in the immediate vicinity of the individual is fine and there is nothing that requires attention. The strained position conversely indicates that cognitive effort is needed: "Cognitive strain is affected by both the level of effort and the presence of unmet demands."[5] Kahneman goes on to explain that our brains do not find cognitive strain particularly enjoyable and that we prefer to be in a state of cognitive ease. By using the aforementioned shortcuts we remain in ease. As Kahneman says, "remember that System 2 is lazy and that mental effort is aversive."[6] He goes so far as to state that ease is related to feelings of familiarity, truth, and goodness, while strain is related to feelings of suspicion, discomfort, and vigilance. No wonder, then, that we would rather rely on our shortcuts.

Overlooked

Kahneman has said that if he could eradicate any of our faulty thought processes, he would target overconfidence.[7] He starts chapter 20 with an account of his time in the Israeli armed forces. He was tasked with designing and delivering accurate screening procedures to predict which candidates would make the best officers. Once the recruits were selected they would go to officer training school, where Kahneman would receive reports on their progress in order to see if his predictions were correct. He found that mostly they were not, saying "The story was always the same: our ability to predict performance at the school was negligible. Our forecasts were better than blind guesses but not by much."[8] It was during this time that Kahneman noticed his first cognitive illusion. He explains that he felt overconfident about the judgments he made regarding his candidates, regardless of the failures that he had already witnessed. He and his colleagues "continued to feel and act as if each of our specific predictions was valid…I coined a term for our experience; the illusion of validity."[9]

While there has been much systemic change to counteract biases and other errors of judgment, overconfidence in our own validity doesn't seem to have been picked up as a major issue by wider institutions. Kahneman gives a telling example of this when he describes finding a no better than chance probability of traders making skilled trades. He presented this finding, calling it the illusion of skill, at a Wall Street dinner he had been invited to, and then "we all went on calmly with our dinners, and I have no doubt that both our findings and their implications were quickly swept under the rug."[10]

Kahneman observes that in the face of information which challenges fundamental aspects of our lives, we are more likely to ignore the facts than to change our behaviors. It may be that some of Kahneman's ideas have been deliberately overlooked, as they are threatening to the reader or the institution that they touch on. One would hope that, as people who study human behavior, psychologists would be immune to such effects, but at several points during *Thinking, Fast and Slow* Kahneman provides evidence to the contrary, stating that even his colleagues specializing in psychology and statistics are prone to System 1 errors.

NOTES

1   Daniel Kahneman, *Thinking, Fast and Slow*, (London: Penguin, 2012), 103.

2   *Thinking, Fast and Slow*, 103.

3   http://www.psychologyconcepts.com/wp-content/uploads/2011/11/muller-lyer-illusion-psychology.jpg.

4   *Thinking, Fast and Slow*, 59

5   *Thinking, Fast and Slow*, 59.

6   *Thinking, Fast and Slow*, 64.

7   David Shariatmadari, "Daniel Kahneman: 'What would I eliminate if I had a magic wand? Overconfidence,'" *Guardian*, July 18 2015.

8   *Thinking, Fast and Slow*, 211.

9   *Thinking, Fast and Slow*, 211.

10 *Thinking, Fast and Slow*, 216.

MODULE 7
ACHIEVEMENT

KEY POINTS

- Kahneman not only presents his own work but also that of his contemporaries, making *Thinking, Fast and Slow* an overall view of the field.

- Kahneman presents us with a number of mental operations that can be seen in all elements of everyday life.

- Although the ideas in *Thinking, Fast and Slow* are widely accepted today, this has not always been the case, particularly among economists.

Assessing the Argument

In the introduction to *Thinking, Fast and Slow*, Kahneman states that his main aim is to introduce a language for talking about thinking. He does this in part by describing his years of experience as an experimental psychologist and as one of the founding fathers of behavioral economics. It is important to note that as a work by a highly cited academic with many published papers, *Thinking, Fast and Slow* brings a whole wealth of peer reviewed scientific thought to the general public. In addition, he synthesizes others' work and theories and explains his ideas in simple language for a general audience. In this sense he is bringing experimental psychology and behavioral economics to a new demographic.

As the book was published relatively recently, we will need to wait and see if Kahneman's new vocabulary takes off in general use; but it has already received many awards. In 2011 it won the Los Angeles Times Book Prize in the Current Interest section.[2] It was also named one of the year's best books in the *New York Times Book Review*,[3] and

> **❝**His central message could not be more important ... human reason left to its own devices is apt to engage in a number of fallacies and systematic errors ... if we want to make better decisions in our personal lives and as a society, we ought to be aware of these biases and seek workarounds. That's a powerful and important discovery.**❞**
>
> Stephen Pinker, *The Guardian*[1]

The Wall Street Journal.[4] In 2012 it won the National Academy of Sciences Best Book Award.[5] In 2013 Kahneman was also awarded the presidential Medal of Freedom which "goes to men and women who have dedicated their own lives to enriching ours[6]" by then President Barack Obama, who said, "This year's honorees have been blessed with extraordinary talent, but what sets them apart is their gift for sharing that talent with the world."[7] Certainly it was Kahneman's aim to share his work with the world, and with such accolades one can hope that his vocabulary will spread.

Achievement in Context

Thinking, Fast and Slow encompasses so many facets of human experience that it is easy to see why it was immediately popular on release. In the current political climate of both Europe and America, marked by rising populism* reliant on simplistic, negative stereotyping* and economic nationalism,* Kahneman shows how such ideology* plays to System 1 thinking. He also notes how political experts often make very wrong assumptions and predictions regarding elections which may, to some extent, explain shocking political events, such as Donald Trump's* presidential victory over Hillary Clinton* in 2016; almost all of the polls had predicted a landslide victory for the latter.

Also in the political sphere, he talks about the halo effect in relation to former US President Barack Obama, stating "If you like the president's politics, you probably like his voice and his appearance as well." He defines the halo effect as "The tendency to like (or dislike) everything about a person—including things you have not observed."[8]

He also demonstrates how such effects can be seen in all fields. Giving an example of the halo effect in his position as a professor, he says "The mechanism was simple: if I had given a high score to the first essay, I gave the student the benefit of the doubt whenever I encountered a vague or ambiguous statement later on."[9] He demonstrates that even those who are aware of these effects need to be vigilant. *Thinking, Fast and Slow* is full of such examples of how System 1 and System 2 affect all spheres of human experience.

Limitations

Daniel Kahneman and his partner Amos Tversky were eventually successful in persuading most people working in the field of psychology and economics that previous notions of how human beings made judgments and decisions were either incorrect or wildly simplistic. This doesn't mean that they didn't have their detractors. These detractors mostly included economists who were followers of the neoclassical school, which promoted the view of rational choice and rational actors, in which people ultimately make logical decisions.

Kahneman and Tversky's theory countered this, but they did not work in deliberate response to neoclassical economists. As Kahneman states in his biographical entry for the Nobel Committee, "If we had intended the article as a challenge to the rational model, we would have written it differently, and the challenge would have been less effective."[10] He goes onto explain that he and Tversky "offered a progress report on our study of judgment under uncertainty. Which included much solid evidence. All inferences about human rationality were drawn by the readers themselves."[11] As is common in *Thinking,*

Fast and Slow, Kahneman trusts his readers, whether they be scientists or the wider general public, to review the evidence and come to their own conclusions. In that sense he always has an answer for any critics; read it and make up your own mind.

That said, after the book was released there was a controversy around some of the experiments on priming effects that Kahneman reported in chapter 4. This means that his assertions based on this evidence need to be re-evaluated.

NOTES

1   The Guardian, "Daniel Kahneman Changed the Way We Think About Thinking. But What Do Other Thinkers Think of Him," *Guardian*, February 16, 2014, accessed September 14, 2017, https://www.theguardian.com/science/2014/feb/16/daniel-kahneman-thinking-fast-and-slow-tributes.

2   http://events.latimes.com/festivalofbooks/book-prizes-winners-by-award/.

3   *The New York Times*, "The Best Books of 2011," November 30th, 2011, retrieved September 1, 2017 http://www.nytimes.com/2011/12/11/books/10-best-books-of-2011.html?mcubz=0.

4   *The Wall Street Journal* "The Best Nonfiction of 2011," December 17th, 2011, retrieved September 1, 2017 https://www.wsj.com/articles/SB10001424052970203518404577097100562141244.

5   *National Academy of Sciences* "Book and Author Talk," April 28th, 2013, retrieved September 1, 2017 http://www.nasonline.org/news-and-multimedia/video-gallery/150th-annual-meeting/book-author-talk/daniel-kahneman.html.

6   *The White House*, "President Obama Names Presidential Medal of Freedom Recipients," August 8th, 2013, retrieved September 1, 2017 https://obamawhitehouse.archives.gov/the-press-office/2013/08/08/president-obama-names-presidential-medal-freedom-recipients.

7   *The White House*, "President Obama Names Presidential Medal of Freedom Recipients."

8   Daniel Kahneman, *Thinking, Fast and Slow*, (London: Penguin, 2012), 82.

9   *Thinking, Fast and Slow*, 83.

10 Daniel Kahneman, "Biographical," Nobelprize.org, accessed August 21, 2016, https://www.nobelprize.org/nobel_prizes/economic-sciences/laureates/2002/kahneman-bio.html.

11 Kahneman, "Biographical."

MODULE 8
PLACE IN THE AUTHOR'S WORK

KEY POINTS

- *Thinking, Fast and Slow* refers to the whole of Kahneman's career, from his time in the army to his current position as Professor Emeritus at Princeton.

- *Thinking, Fast and Slow* is a new canon of work in the field of judgment and decision-making.

- *Thinking, Fast and Slow* presents new evidence, making it an addition to Kahneman's previous work.

Positioning

Thinking, Fast and Slow is Kahneman's latest work. It represents the culmination of a lifetime of research in cognitive psychology and statistics. Kahneman started his career looking at potential army officers and devising methods by which they could be predicted to perform well in their roles. He was also intensely interested in the statistical methods by which one could form such predictions. Interestingly, his main assertions from this period focus on how confused he was that such predictions were incorrect.

Perhaps the most significant result of his work with Amos Tversky was prospect theory, which describes how people make decisions when risk is involved, and argues that although it might seem intuitive to assert that humans make rational decisions under such circumstances, this is not actually the case. During this period Kahneman and Tversky also published "Judgment Under Uncertainty: Heuristics and Biases,"[2] a seminal work in the field of behavioral economics. It was this work for which he was awarded the Nobel Memorial Prize in Economics in 2002.

> ❝ I had limited ambitions, I didn't aspire to great success. I was very hardworking, but I didn't expect to be a famous psychologist. ❞
> Daniel Kahneman, *The Guardian* [1]

The focus of Kahneman's work then became hedonic psychology, or the psychology of happiness. It is important to note, however, that while this may appear to represent a shift in academic focus, Kahneman's work was still primarily centered on judgment and decision-making. An example of this is his concept of the focusing illusion.* He developed this theory while observing that people focus on one differing aspect when making judgments. He asked participants in an experiment "Does living in California make people happy?" and found that they would usually say yes, thinking of California's good weather and ignoring the multitude of factors that might negate its influence. Thus, his participants "focused" on one aspect when making a judgment.

Integration

The five sections of *Thinking, Fast and Slow* broadly represent the stages that Kahneman progressed through in his academic career. He has occasionally dabbled in areas that may seem slightly different to his overall interest in judgment and decision-making, such as his foray into cognitive pupillometry* with Jackson Beatty.* Using this research method, a researcher can observe how much attention a participant is paying to a task by pupil size. However, he always manages to relate the strands of his work back to his main theories and thus integrate such research into a larger canon of ideas. His two system routes—fast and slow, 1 and 2, or intuitive and deliberate—add another level of understanding to his earlier work on biases, heuristics, and effects. For example, when discussing the relevance of cognitive pupillometry to his work, Kahneman explains that the size of the pupil is related to whether System 1 or System 2 is in charge (the pupils dilate when one is paying attention to a task, hence System 2 is operating).

The two-system theory lends a level of coherence to all of his previous work, in that it explains neatly how and why errors of judgment occur while offering new insights into hedonic psychology using a well-understood paradigm. Perhaps unsurprisingly, Kahneman looks at how we remember happiness versus how we experience it, another type of dual process. He focuses on how certain aspects of experience affect judgment about that experience, highlighting that often we judge quality of life via small slices of time in which positive or negative emotion is present rather than assessing life as a whole. We are still making errors of judgment.

Significance

Daniel Kahneman has had such a long and illustrious career that it is difficult to say which of his works are the most significant. *Thinking, Fast and Slow*, while presenting that work as an integrated corpus, also shifts from his normal intended audience of academics, economists, and scientists, trying to attract a wider public of popular science readers. It also sees him reporting the results of his contemporaries and colleagues and highlighting their significant theories and experiments.

An example of this is the gorilla experiment by Christopher Chabris* and Daniel Simons.* They demonstrated selective attention by asking participants to count how many times a basketball was passed between players wearing white. They showed that participants were so focused on this task, they didn't notice that halfway through the experiment a man dressed as a gorilla walked in between the players, beat his chest and then walked away.[3] In this sense, the book is a history of the field of judgment and decision-making and behavioral economics as well as a review of Kahneman's work.

Kahneman also uses *Thinking, Fast and Slow* to address newer issues in the field of judgment and decision-making. He looks at accurate intuitions as well as errors for the first time, particularly among experts such as chess masters. He also explains how emotion plays a much larger role in decision-making that he had previously hypothesized. He uses the example of terrorism to demonstrate that when we have strong emotions towards an event it becomes much more "available," meaning we will overestimate the probability of such an event occurring again.

Kahneman also provides as appendices the full text of two publications co-authored by Amos Tversky, one on prospect theory, and the other the essay "Judgment Under Uncertainty," which is widely accepted as the founding text of behavioral economics. The inclusion of these two academic papers show that while this book is for a wide and global audience, it is also for scholars, and is firmly rooted in a canon of work which Kahneman was influential in shaping. As such, although much of the book brings new evidence into Kahneman's theories on how people think, it still represents a compendium of and an addition to the work he has contributed to the scientific community since the beginning of his academic career.

NOTES

1   David Shariatmadari, "Daniel Kahneman: 'What would I eliminate if I had a magic wand? Overconfidence,'" *Guardian*, July 18 2015.

2   Amos Tversky and Daniel Kahneman. "Judgment under uncertainty: Heuristics and biases." In *Utility, probability, and human decision-making*, eds. Dirk Wendt and C.A. Vlek (Netherlands: Springer, 1975), 141-162.

3   Daniel Kahneman, *Thinking, Fast and Slow*, (London: Penguin, 2012), 23-24.

SECTION 3
IMPACT

MODULE 9
THE FIRST RESPONSES

KEY POINTS

*   *Thinking, Fast and Slow* was generally well received and won many awards.

*   Kahneman got caught up in the "Replication Crisis"* as some of the research he had reported, particularly on priming, came under scrutiny.

*   As a result of a subsequent controversy, Kahneman publicly voiced his concerns and revised his opinion.

Criticism

Thinking, Fast and Slow made the *New York Times* Best Seller List and won many awards. Initial reviews of the work were glowing. Roger Lowenstein proclaimed it a "monumental achievement" in Bloomberg,[1] and an article in *The Economist* stated that "As Copernicus removed the Earth from the centre of the universe and Darwin knocked humans off their biological perch, Mr Kahneman has shown that we are not the paragons of reason we assume ourselves to be."[2] Distinguished scholar of behavioral economics Richard Thaler* said, "Buy it fast. Read it slowly. It will change the way you think."[3]

Not all reviews, however, were entirely positive. In an article for the *Huffington Post* titled "Thinking, fast and slow and poorly and well," the economist and academic David K. Levine stated that the book was tedious and lacking intellectual substance. He went on, "The theme is that people are full of biases—that economists believe otherwise and so are full of it. I imagine this is a popular message."[4] He also found the book "remarkably smug," with "some strange historical oversights."[5] However, as Kahneman has been known to disagree with

> **❝ I have changed my views about the size of behavioral priming effects – they cannot be as large and as robust as my chapter suggested. ❞**
>
> Daniel Kahneman, *Reconstruction of a Train Wreck: How Priming Research Went off the Rails*

economists, particularly those who do not subscribe to behavioral economics, Levine may have taken offense. It is also noteworthy that in the above-mentioned article Levine promoted his own book *Is Behavioral Economics Doomed*,[6] a title that may suggest the author's own biases.

Responses

Chapter 4 of *Thinking, Fast and Slow* is concerned with priming effects,* which suggest that people can be influenced, even subconsciously, to behave in specific ways if they are exposed to certain stimuli. Kahneman describes these results as surprisingly robust and states "Disbelief is not an option. The results are not made up, nor are they statistical flukes. You have no choice but to accept that the major conclusions of these studies are true."[7]

In 2012, however, Doyen and colleagues failed to replicate one of the studies reported by Kahneman, in which participants exposed to (or primed with) ideas of old age slowed down their walking speed.[8] This worried Kahneman enough to write an open letter to the author of the original study, John Bargh,* in which he complained "Your field is now the poster child for doubts about the integrity of psychological research." He was obviously worried about his own reporting of these results, as he also wrote that his issue was not regarding those who had expressed doubts but "with the much larger population of colleagues who in the past accepted your surprising results as facts when they were published," and it seems like he is addressing his critics by going on to say that "These people have now attached a question mark to the field, and it is your responsibility to remove it …. My reason for writing this letter is that I see a train wreck looming."[9]

Conflict and Consensus

Summing up the controversy over priming effects, in 2017 Schimmack*, Heene*, and Kesavan* state, while criticizing Kahneman in a blog post titled "Reconstruction of a Train Wreck: How Priming Research Went off the Rails,"[10] that he "should not consider the presented studies as scientific evidence that subtle cues in [subjects'] environment can have strong effects on their behavior outside their awareness."[11] Kahneman responds directly to these criticisms in a comment in the blogs reply section. In the comment he shows that he understands that "the results of priming studies were based on small samples, that the effect sizes were perhaps implausibly large, and that no single study was conclusive on its own," thereby taking responsibility for his participation in the scandal. He justifies having taken that position, stating "What impressed me was the unanimity and coherence of the results reported by many laboratories. I concluded that priming effects are easy for skilled experimenters to induce."[12] Ultimately he admits that "I now understand that my reasoning was flawed and that I should have known better."[13]

Kahneman explains the notion of overconfidence repeatedly in *Thinking, Fast and Slow*. When he states that *he* should know better it is because he gives plenty of examples where even scientists and academics such as himself are swayed by biases in the face of information that supports their own theoretical leanings. He is therefore uniquely placed to revise his conclusions. Unfortunately the replication crisis is still unfolding, with other major academics coming under attack.

NOTES

1   Roger Lowenstein "Book Review: Thinking, Fast and Slow by Daniel Kahneman," *Bloomberg* October 28, 2011, retrieved August 22, 2017 https://www.bloomberg.com/news/articles/2011-10-27/book-review-thinking-fast-and-slow-by-daniel-kahneman.

2   *The Economist* "Not So Smart Now" October 9 2011, retrieved September 12, 2017 http://www.economist.com/node/21534752.

3   Daniel Kahneman, *Thinking, Fast and Slow*, (London: Penguin, 2012).

4   David K. Levine "Thinking, Fast and Slow and Poorly and Well" *The Huffington Post* September 22, 2012, retrieved August 22, 2017 http://www.huffingtonpost.com/david-k-levine/thinking-fast-and-slow-an_b_1906061.html.

5   David K. Levine "Thinking, Fast and Slow and Poorly and Well" *The Huffington Post* September 22, 2012, retrieved August 22, 2017 http://www.huffingtonpost.com/david-k-levine/thinking-fast-and-slow-an_b_1906061.html.

6   David K. Levine, *Is Behavioral Economics Doomed?: The Ordinary Versus the Extraordinary* (Cambridge: Open Book Publishers, 2012).

7   Daniel Kahneman, *Thinking, Fast and Slow*, (London: Penguin, 2012), 57.

8   Stéphane Doyen, Olivier Klein, Cora-Lise Pichon, and Axel Cleeremans. "Behavioral priming: it's all in the mind, but whose mind?." *Plosone* 7, no. 1 (2012).

9   Available online from http://www.nature.com/polopoly_fs/7.6716.1349271308!/suppinfoFile/Kahneman%20Letter.pdf.

10 Ulrich Schimmack, Moritz Heene, and Kamini Kesavan "Reconstruction of a Train Wreck: How Priming Research Went off the Rails" Replicability Index February 2, 2017, retrieved August 22, 2017 https://replicationindex.wordpress.com/2017/02/02/reconstruction-of-a-train-wreck-how-priming-research-went-of-the-rails/.

11 Schimmack et al., "Reconstruction of a Train Wreck."

12 Schimmack et al., "Reconstruction of a Train Wreck."

13 Schimmack et al., "Reconstruction of a Train Wreck."

MODULE 10
THE EVOLVING DEBATE

KEY POINTS

- Daniel Kahneman has influenced many thinkers across many different schools of thought.

- He is known as one of the founding fathers of the behavioral economic school of thought.

- His relationship with Amos Tversky was memorialized in the 2016 non-fiction book *The Undoing Project: A Friendship that Changed the World.*[1]

Uses and Problems

Kahneman's work consistently asks other people to think about thinking. In *Thinking, Fast and Slow* he does this for a popular audience, but his published academic work has asked the same of contemporaries, collaborators, opponents, and the wider scientific community. Stephen Pinker is one of the world's most famous psychologists and a Harvard professor. He remembers Kahneman noting at a presentation "that the idea of human nature with inherent flaws was consistent with a tragic view of the human condition and it's a part of being human that we have to live with that tragedy,"[2] and has said that this observation has informed much of his work since. Pinker's latest book, *The Better Angels of our Nature*,[3] is partly concerned with how we don't think statistically about the fact that rates of violence have been declining. He claims that Kahneman has presented a paradigm through which the public can view his own work.

Richard Thaler and Cass Sunstein,* authors of the 2008 book *Nudge,* have also been guided by Kahneman and Tversky. They define a nudge as "any aspect of the choice architecture that alters people's

> ❝Danny is a fertile source of ideas. So he's really
> generative… Danny is off-the-charts generative. He's
> almost the poetic or novelistic mind in the room. And
> Amos is the diamond cutter. Amos is a pure analytical
> mind, who sees levels of abstraction in Danny's ideas
> and generalizes them and formalizes them.❞
> Michael Lewis, *The Guardian*

behaviour in a predictable way without forbidding any options or
significantly changing their economic incentives."[4] For example,
"Putting fruit at eye level counts as a nudge. Banning junk food does
not."[5] Of working with Kahneman and Tversky, Thaler has stated that
"They knew nothing about economics and I knew nothing about
psychology, so it was one step at a time, but we had a lot of fun."[6]

Kahneman is known to be kind to younger researchers and
promote their work if he agrees with it, which is why he mentions
Nassim Taleb's *The Black Swan* often throughout *Thinking, Fast and
Slow.* Taleb recounts the first time that he met Kahneman at a
conference where the presentation of his work *The Black Swan* was
not well received: "I feared that they would disinvite me from the rest
of the conference, and perhaps even throw me out of the building, and
if they could, the country."[7] Thankfully for Taleb, Kahneman was next
to present, and "He unexpectedly saved [Taleb's] life when his opening
sentence was that he 'fully agreed with the previous speaker.'"[8]

Kahneman's work will likely continue to influence the world's
foremost thinkers in his field and beyond.

Schools of Thought

In his 1976 work *The Economic Approach to Human Behavior,*[9] Gary
Becker* argues that people make rational, logical decisions designed
to maximize gain when faced with economic choices and that this

model could be applied to all aspects of other human action. Although the neoclassical economists had upheld that people are rational actors who make rational decisions, there were some notable concessions that psychological factors were important in economic modeling. The idea of "bounded rationality" put forward by Simon in the 1950s had growing traction with some in the field. Kahneman and Tversky demonstrated this using decision tasks such as the one below.

- Decision (I): Choose between
  - A. A sure gain of $240
  - B. 25% chance to gain $1000 and a 75% chance to gain nothing
- Decision (II): Choose between
  - C. A sure loss of $750
  - D. A 75% chance to lose $1000 and a 25% chance to lose nothing[10]

They found that people made decisions based on how the choice was framed. Framed as a gain, people tended to choose option A. Framed as a loss, people tended to choose option D. These insights and collaborations with economist Richard Thaler were the foundation of a new school of thought, behavioral economics, which recognizes that psychological and social factors impact economic judgments and decision-making.

In Current Scholarship

Kahneman and Tvesrsky's friendship and collaboration was so profound that in 2016 it became the subject of a non-fiction book written by Michael Lewis. Lewis has previously written about rare economic events such as the 2008 financial crash in *The Big Short*[11] and is a *New York Times* bestselling author. In his book *The Undoing Project: A Friendship that Changed our Minds*, Lewis chronicles how the pair met and the story of their incredibly productive time together. He also shows us how different they were, and that it is remarkable that "two so radically different personalities could find common ground, much less become soul mates."[12] Tversky was an impeccably organized optimist, and Kahneman a worrier, a consummate pessimist, and famously messy. "Danny was a Holocaust kid; Amos a swaggering Sabra—the slang term for a native Israeli ... Danny was always sure he was wrong. Amos was always sure he was right."[13]

Lewis describes their relationship like a marriage, and as such sometimes conflicted. This culminated with Kahneman at one point writing to Tversky to cut off all contact with him. He reversed this decision 3 days later when Tversky called him to say that he had melanoma and only 6 months to live. The two men remained friends until the end of Tversky's life in 1996.

NOTES

1 Michael Lewis. *The Undoing Project: A Friendship that Changed the World* (London: Penguin, 2016).

2 The Guardian, "Daniel Kahneman Changed the Way We Think About Thinking. But What Do Other Thinkers Think of Him," *Guardian*, February 16, 2014, accessed September 14, 2017, https://www.theguardian.com/science/2014/feb/16/daniel-kahneman-thinking-fast-and-slow-tributes.

3 Steven Pinker *The Better Angels of Our Nature: The Decline of Violence in History and its Causes* (London: Penguin, 2011).

4 Richard Thaler and Cass Sunstein, *Nudge: The Gentle Power of Choice Architecture* (New Haven, Conn.: Yale, 2008), 6.

5 Thaler and Sunstein, *Nudge*, 6.

6 The Guardian, "Daniel Kahneman Changed the Way We Think."

7 The Guardian, "Daniel Kahneman Changed the Way We Think."

8 The Guardian, "Daniel Kahneman Changed the Way We Think."

9   Gary Becker. *The Economic Approach to Human Behavior* (Chicago: University of Chicago, 2013).

10   Daniel Kahneman, *Thinking, Fast and Slow* (London: Penguin, 2012), 334.

11   Michael Lewis *The Big Short: Inside the Doomsday Machine* (London: Penguin, 2011).

12   Michael Lewis. *The Undoing Project*, chapter 5.

13   Michael Lewis. *The Undoing Project*, chapter 5.

MODULE 11
IMPACT AND INFLUENCE TODAY

KEY POINTS

- Kahneman is one of the world's most influential psychologists. He has impacted many fields, including hedonic psychology.
- Kahneman is objective in his assessment of potential opponents.
- Kahneman believes that the future of psychology lies in cognitive neuroscience.*

Position

It is hard to estimate the overall influence of the work that Kahneman reports in *Thinking, Fasting and Slow*. He has already influenced schools such as psychology, economics, sociology, politics, law, and even helped kick start a new one, behavioral economics. His influence also shows in the 2013 world happiness report published by the respected British economist Professor Richard Layard.* The study of happiness is often the domain of self-help books or eastern wisdom tutorials, but Layard said of Kahneman's influence, "Danny Kahneman changed my life. He persuaded me that happiness is a real experience which can be measured and therefore studied and understood."[1] Layard had, before meeting Kahneman, devoted his career to the study of inequality and unemployment but he says "I had always believed that the best society is one where there is the most happiness and (above all) the least misery."[2] Layard became one of the first-ever economists to study happiness and was directly influenced by Kahneman as he says "the new science of happiness, which Danny was inspiring, made this ideal a hundred times more practicable."[3] Kahneman's work and his

> **❝** I've called Daniel Kahneman the world's most
> influential living psychologist and I believe that is
> true. He pretty much created the field of behavioural
> economics and has revolutionised large parts of cognitive
> psychology and social psychology. **❞**
>
> Stephen Pinker, *The Guardian*

influence is so widely seen as seminal that *Thinking, Fast and Slow*
represents a shift of audience rather than a shift in how well he and his
work are regarded.

Interaction

As a Nobel Laureate, or academically, not many have made a similar
impact in as many fields as Daniel Kahneman. His work was contrasted
with that of the popular science writer Malcolm Gladwell,*
particularly in relation to Gladwell's 2008 book *Blink: The Power of
Thinking without Thinking*.[4] The premise of *Blink* is that intuition is
incredibly powerful and people are capable of making amazing and
accurate decisions subconsciously. He uses examples such as surgeons
who have to make snap decisions in order to save a life on the
operating table, often in the absence of objective knowledge as to how
that decision will pan out. Critics of this approach to decision-making
such as Maria Popova have stated that he was essentially arguing that
intuition was some kind of force or magic and his premise was anti-
scientific. When reviewing *Thinking, Fast and Slow* in *The Atlantic* she
called it "Anti Gladwellian."[5] Kahneman looks at intuition as a series
of memory activations. He explains how someone who appears to
make impressive expert intuitive decisions has practiced making such
judgments so often they have a well-honed shortcut for doing so. In
this sense good intuition among experts is essentially a System 1
process. Able to take such a view on this issue, in a 2012 interview he

clarified his position on "Blink" stating that although he felt Gladwell does not believe that intuition equals magic, "his story has helped people, in a belief that they want to have, which is that intuition works magically; and that belief, is false."[6] Kahneman is able to separate the true intentions of his apparent opponents from the wider public impact that they have. His issue with Gladwell is not that he is anti-scientific but that his message is taken as such.

The Continuing Debate

Relations between Kahneman and his critic Gerd Gigerenzer are more acrimonious. Gigerenzer's 2014 book *Risk Savvy: How to make good decisions*[7] saw him use a chapter to attempt to dismantle the theories suggested in *Thinking, Fast and Slow*, although he never names Kahneman outright as the main proponent of these ideas. It is important to note, however, that while they disagree on some aspects, Gigerenzer also relies on heuristics as an explanatory tool. It could be argued that one of the main premises of *Thinking, Fast and Slow* is persuading people to be more risk savvy; it has just used a different language to do so.

When directly asked where he sees the future of the field going, Kahneman responded that he looks to the research choices of students, which indicates that neuroscience, drawing on brain research and psychology, is the next step in understanding cognition. One problem with Kahneman's argument is that, as he tells us, System 1 and System 2 are fictional characters. They are conceptual, not objectively visible. This is problematic in a discipline which is increasingly concerned with the specific neuroarchitecture of thought, trying to discover which neural regions and pathways are responsible for what behaviors. Kahneman also notes that "Signs of emotional arousal are salient in the reactions to many events—and especially to decisions—so the conceptual separation between emotion and pure cognition seems likely to crumble."[8] In the future, he implies, we will be able to chart the neural flow of both emotional thought and higher-functioning thought, such as paying attention to a task. In response to a question regarding which topics he wished he'd been able to address in his career, Kahneman replied, "I sometimes wish I were 20 years younger—I would have switched to brain research."[9] The future may lie in such research, given that brain imaging technology is improving year on year. It maybe that at some point we can chart System 1 and System 2 thoughts using such technology, and Kahneman's influence will spread further.

NOTES

1   The Guardian, "Daniel Kahneman Changed the Way We Think About Thinking. But What Do Other Thinkers Think of Him," *Guardian*, February 16, 2014, accessed September 14, 2017, https://www.theguardian.com/science/2014/feb/16/daniel-kahneman-thinking-fast-and-slow-tributes.

2   The Guardian, "Daniel Kahneman Changed the Way We Think."

3   The Guardian, "Daniel Kahneman Changed the Way We Think."

4   Malcolm Gladwell, *Blink: The power of thinking without thinking* (Boston: Back Bay Books, 2007).

5   Maria Popova, "The Anti-Gladwell: Kahneman's New Way to Think About Thinking" *The Atlantic* November 1, 2011, retrieved September 6, 2017, https://www.theatlantic.com/health/archive/2011/11/the-anti-gladwell-kahnemans-new-way-to-think-about-thinking/247407/.

6   The Charlie Rose Show: https://charlierose.com/videos/15620. Accessed September 12, 2017.

7   Gerd Gigerenzer, *Risk Savvy: How to Make Good Decisions* (London: Penguin, 2014).

8   http://freakonomics.com/2011/11/28/daniel-kahneman-answers-your-questions/.

9   http://freakonomics.com/2011/11/28/daniel-kahneman-answers-your-questions/.

MODULE 12
WHERE NEXT?

KEY POINTS

- *Thinking, Fast and Slow* has the potential to revolutionize how we think about thinking.

- Kahneman's many disciples also propagate many similar theories and seek to enlighten us as to how the mind works.

- *Thinking, Fast and Slow* is essential reading for anyone who is interested in human behavior and action.

Potential

Bringing Kahneman's wealth of experience in understanding not only how people think, but how and why they make errors of thinking to a global audience has a huge potential to affect behavior. In the book he gives examples demonstrating cognitive errors and biases such as: judges making harsher decisions before lunch when they are hungry; highly skilled financial traders performing no better than random chance; how stereotyping doesn't represent true information about an individual; how we are often overconfident; how we are risk averse; how our experience and memory can be completely discordant; and how we often make ourselves the best story possible out of what we have in front of us and believe it to be the truth—and those are just a few examples from *Thinking, Fast and Slow*. What makes Kahneman unique is his approach to his own work; he not only explains these mental operations, he also gives examples of how his own faulty thinking gave rise to such theories in the first place. Where most of us don't want to be wrong, Kahneman looks at such errors with curiosity, and as an opportunity

> ❝Kahneman, a winner of the Nobel Prize for Economics, distils a lifetime of research into an encyclopaedic coverage of both the surprising miracles and the equally surprising mistakes of our conscious and subconscious thinking. He achieves an even greater miracle by weaving his insights into an engaging narrative that is compulsively readable from beginning to end.❞
>
> William Easterly, *The Financial Times*

for furthering understanding of the workings of the mind. Potentially, with the increasing sophistication of neuroimaging techniques, Kahneman's routes could be made manifest, and we might be able to see the thought processes he describes as neurons seen travelling in different patterns through the brain.

Future Directions

Kahneman has many disciples, most of whom have also become well known, at least in their own disciplines. A few have become household names, either due to promotion from Kahneman, as in the case of Nassim Taleb, or due to their own forays into popular science, such as Stephen Dubner* and Stephen Levitt,* who co-authored the popular *Freakonomics* series, or Richard Thaler and Cass Sunstein, co-authors of the book *Nudge* and long-time collaborators and colleagues of both Kahneman and Tversky. Dan Ariely,* an Israeli American polymath who was also mentored by and collaborated with Kahneman, is now a well-known name due to his popular science books *Predictably Irrational,*[1] *The Upside of Irrationality,*[2] and *The Honest Truth about Dishonesty,*[3] all published since 2008 and all *New York Times* best sellers. He has also appeared as a TED* speaker and writes a column for the Wall Street Journal. In 2015 his book *The Honest Truth about Dishonesty* was turned into a film and he is currently a professor in behavioral science at Duke University.

In *Predictably Irrational*, Ariely writes, "My goal, by the end of this book, is to help you fundamentally rethink what makes you and the people around you tick," adding "Once you see how systematic certain mistakes are—how we repeat them again and again—I think you will begin to learn how to avoid some of them."[4] Kahneman's goal of creating a new way of talking and thinking is echoed by his contemporaries and those he has mentored. One hopes that between them, at some point, there will be a popular vernacular to more accurately describe human behavior.

Summary

There are few works that are not only likely to become textbooks for undergraduates in a variety of disciplines (in the case of *Thinking, Fast and* Slow, psychology and economics at least) but which are also a *New York Times* number 1 bestsellers in the genre of popular science. There are fewer still written by Nobel Laureates. The importance of bringing an understanding of such a key factor of psychological life—the way we think, how we think and why we make errors—into popular distribution, cannot be underestimated.

Anyone who is interested in why they make the decisions they do should read this book. It is a wonderful way to understand ourselves and to make sure that the choices and judgments we make are based on evidence rather than the lazy parts of our brains, which don't really want to do any hard work. These lessons are useful both in personal and professional life. The book also gives us a framework to view the messages we receive from advertisers, the political class, and others, allowing us to check that our System 1s are not being manipulated. On a grander scale, *Thinking, Fast and Slow* demonstrates that we need to ensure that judgments and decisions made societally that affect the lives of the population are not subject to System 1 errors.

NOTES

1   Dan Ariely, *Predictably Irrational* (New York: HarperCollins, 2008).

2   Dan Ariely and Simon Jones, *The Upside of Irrationality* (New York: HarperCollins, 2010).

3   Dan Ariely and Simon Jones, *The (Honest) Truth About Dishonesty: How We Lie to Everyone, Especially Ourselves*, Vol. 336 (New York: HarperCollins, 2012).

4   Ariely, *Predictably Irrational*, 12.

GLOSSARY

GLOSSARY OF TERMS

9/11: This is short hand for the terrorist attack that happened on September 11, 2001. Terrorists flew planes into the Twin Towers in New York, resulting in their total collapse and thousands of deaths.

2008 Financial Crash: Brought about by the unregulated selling of sub-prime mortgages in the US. Many of the world's big banks were affected, leading some, such as Lehman Brothers, to collapse. The fallout was a near-global recession.

Adversarial Collaborations: A term coined by Daniel Kahneman to describe working with one's opponents on a shared research project.

Affect Heuristic: Relates to the influence that positive or negative emotion has on judgments and decision-making.

American Psychological Association (APA): Formed in 1892, the APA is the organization that represents those working in Psychological Science in the United States.

Associative Memory: The memory system that is representative of the relationships between things. For example, seeing your friend and knowing what she looks like and what her name is happens when your associative memory is functioning.

Behavioral Economics: The science of how psychological, cognitive, and social factors affect value-based decision-making. For example, it seeks to explain why one might assign a price to something based on its sentimental rather than absolute value.

Bias: A leaning towards or against something based on assumptions or stereotypes.

Cognition: Thought.

Cognitive Ease: Ease of thought.

Cognitive Neuroscience: The science of the biological apparatus underlying cognition.**Cognitive Psychology:** The psychology of thought.

Cognitive Pupillometry: The study of thought-related pupil movement.

Cognitive Strain: Difficulty of thought.**Confederate:** In experimental psychology, a person who is allied with the researcher, often without other participants' knowledge.

Confirmation Bias: The tendency to believe things that fit in with our worldview and reject that which threatens it.

D-Day: June 6, 1944, when the Allies launched a major attack to reclaim occupied territory from the Nazis in World War II.

Dual Processing Theory: The idea that thought occurs via two different processes, often a subconscious one and a conscious one.

Economic Nationalism: An ideology that focuses on putting national financial interests ahead of other economic concerns.

Effect: In psychology, a replicable phenomenon.

Experiencing Self: The self that is in the moment, receiving all present sensory input.

Fallacy: A believed falsehood.

Focusing Illusion: When people pay attention to only one aspect of a decision when making a judgment.

Framing Effect: How one can affect the outcome of a decision by changing the way in which it is presented.

Halo Effect: The likelihood that previously good memories will influence how we view a person in subsequent interactions.

Hedonic Psychology: The psychology of happiness. For example, studying which countries in the world are happiest and why, or finding barriers to happiness in married couples.

Heuristic: A mental shortcut or "rule of thumb."

Holocaust: The systematic extermination of Jewish people ordered by Nazi leader Adolf Hitler, in the run up to and during World War II, resulting in an estimated 6 million deaths.

Ideology: A system of ideas or beliefs which affects a person's approach to life or professional work.

Illusion: Something that appears to be real when it is not. It can relate to visual illusions such as mirages or cognitive illusions such as the illusion of skill.

Illusion of Skill: When luck masquerades as skill.

Interpretation of Dreams: 1899 work by Sigmund Freud in which he explains that our dreams are full of messages sent by our subconscious and we can interpret them if we understand certain psychoanalytic factors.

Israeli Defense Forces: The military arm of the Israel Security Forces; it encompasses ground forces, air forces and the navy.

Law of Least Effort: The idea that your mind will opt for whatever assumption/ conclusion is the easiest to come to.

Mere Exposure Effect: Being exposed to something, no matter how briefly, will predispose favorable judgments of it in subsequent encounters.

Muller-Lyer Illusion: A visual illusion whereby the placement of arrows either towards or away from a line makes the line look bigger or smaller when in fact it is the same length.

Naturalistic Decision Making (NMD): School of thought put forward against the ideas of Kahneman and Tversky. Argues that decision-making isn't formulaic and can't be studied using experimental protocols.

Negative Stereotyping: Beliefs about a group of people based on negative assumptions, for example from the media.

Neoclassical School of Economics: A school of thought emerging in the 1860s, interested in the attribution of resources in resource-scarce environments. It introduced the concept of utility function, which is the amount of satisfaction we derive from an item, and production function, which is how much of an item can be produced. The neoclassical school argued that when faced with utility and production, consumers would behave rationally and make decisions based on functionality.

Nobel Prize: Award given annually in the name of Swedish inventor Alfred Nobel, which recognizes the pinnacle of achievement in a given discipline. Recipients are known as Nobel Laureates.

Nuremberg Trials: Military trials held between November 20, 1945 and October 1, 1946 of key personnel in the Nazi party accused of crimes against humanity.

Planning Fallacy: The false optimism felt in the planning stages of a project, often relating to the time the project will realistically take.

Populism: A political approach in which the concerns of regular people or "the populace" are emphasized.

Presidential Medal of Freedom: The highest civilian award that can be bestowed in the United States.

Priming Effects: Exposing someone to an idea before asking them to perform in a certain way will change their performance.

Professor Emeritus: A professor who is retired but is still affiliated with the institution. Often these are academics that have made a significant contribution to the faculty.

Prospect Theory: Theory proposed by Daniel Kahneman and Amos Tversky that argues that people make decisions based on perceived gain and losses.

Rational Agent Theory: The idea promoted by the neoclassical economists that when faced with economic decisions people act logically to maximize potential outcome.

Remembering Self: The part of the self that records and organizes personal history.

Replicability: In psychology, the ability to replicate an experiment and get similar results. It is one of the hallmarks of good experimental protocol.

Replication Crisis: The controversy, kicking off about 2011, around a number of seminal experiements in psychology that could not be replicated.

TED: Stands for Technology, Education and Design. TED is an organization that holds conferences with influential speakers on a variety of topics. Most are now available to watch online freely.

What You See Is All There Is (WYSIATI): The idea that we make up a story that best fits the information we have available to us at the time, and then believe that the story is true.

World War II: A global conflict that was started when Germany invaded Poland in 1939. It involved 30 countries that broadly split into two opposing sides, the Allies (including the UK, France, the Soviet Union and America) and the Axis (including Germany, Italy and Japan) and lasted until 1945. It was the bloodiest war in modern history, with top fatality estimates of 85 million people.

PEOPLE MENTIONED IN THE TEXT

Dan Ariely (b. 1967) is an Israeli American professor of psychology and behavioral economics at Duke University. His TED talks have been viewed more than 10 million times and he is the author of several popular behavioral economics books including *Predictably Irrational*.

Solomon Asch (1907–96) was a Polish-born social and experimental psychologist who was well known for his conformity experiments, in which he showed that when questioned under enough pressure people would conform to incorrect answers rather than defend their own correct ones.

John Bargh (b. 1955) is social psychologist at Yale University. He is particularly interested in priming effects. Recently, he was caught in a controversy regarding the replicability of his experiments.

Jackson Beatty is Professor Emeritus in behavioral neuroscience at UCLA and founding father of the field of cognitive pupillometry.

Christopher Chabris (b. 1966) is an American-born research psychologist and associate professor of psychology and co-director of the neuroscience program at Union College, New York. He is best known for co-authoring *The Invisible Gorilla*.

Hilary Clinton (b. 1947) was a presidential candidate in 2008 and 2016 and First Lady of the United States from 1993–2001.

Stephen Dubner (b. 1963) is an American journalist who taught at the University of Columbia and was also an editor for the New York

Times. He is best known as the co-author of the popular science/
economics book *Freakonomics*.

Sigmund Freud (1856–1939) was the father of psychoanalysis,
which he devised as a way to understand the maladies of the human
mind, an interest he turned to after training as a medical doctor. He
was the first to suggest that there is an unknown component to our
minds that works automatically. His theories are still taught and argued
over today.

Gerd Gigerenzer (b. 1947) is a German psychologist who studies
risk, judgment and decision-making. He is the currently the director
of the Center for Adaptive Behavior and Cognition (ABC) at the Max
Planck Institute for Human Development, and of the Harding Center
for Risk Literacy.

Malcolm Gladwell (b. 1963) is a British Canadian journalist and
author who is best known for writing about social sciences for a
popular audience. All of his published books have made the New York
Times best seller list.

Moritz Heene is a professor of psychology with a special interest in
methodology at Ludwig-Maximilians Universität München.

Kamini Kesavan (b. 1991) is a business analyst at Metafinanz
Informationssysteme GmbH and a former Masters student at Ludwig-
Maximilians Universität München

Gary Klein (b. 1944) is an American-born psychologist best known
for his work in the field of Naturalistic Decision Making.

Richard Layard (b. 1934) is a British economist and co-author of the World Happiness Report and Program Director of the Centre for Economic Performance at the London School of Economics.

Yeshayahu Leibowitz (1903–94) was a Russian Jewish polymath who lectured in subjects such as philosophy and biochemistry at the Hebrew University of Jerusalem, where he taught for nearly 60 years.

Stephen Levitt (b. 1967) is Distinguished Professor of economics and director of the Becker Center on Chicago Price Theory at the University of Chicago. Levitt is well known for his unique take on economic phenomena as the co-author of the popular science/ economics book *Freakonomics*.

Kurt Lewin (1890–1947) was a German American psychologist widely held to be the founder of social psychology due to his applied psychology approach. He lectured at various academic establishments including MIT, Cornell, and Duke.

Michael Lewis (b. 1960) is a best-selling author and financial journalist who writes about unexpected or interesting aspects of economics.

Paul Meehl (1920–2003) was a respected clinical psychologist and recipient of many awards, including the APA's Award for Lifetime Contributions to Psychology in 1996. He spent most of his academic career at the University of Minnesota. He argued that applying statistics to predictions of behavior would be more lucrative than clinical assessment.

Stanley Milgram (1933–84) was an American social and experimental psychologist. He was best known for his notorious experiments on obedience, in which he showed that, contrary to popular opinion, people would obey an authority figure even if it meant seriously hurting another individual.

Barack Obama (b. 1961) served as the 44th president of the United States between 2009 and 2017.

David Rapaport (1911–60) was a Hungarian clinical psychologist and psychoanalyst. He was best known for attempting to measure psychoanalytic properties metrically.

Ulrich Schimmack is a professor of psychology at the University of Toronto, specializing in hedonic psychology.

Herbert Simon (1916–2001) was awarded the Turing Award in 1975 and the Nobel Prize in Economics in 1978. Simon was a renowned polymath whose work straddled disciplines such as cognitive psychology, artificial intelligence, and business.

Daniel Simons (b. 1969) is a professor in psychology at the Beckman Institute for Advanced Science and Technology at the University of Illinois, best known for his work on attention and for co-authoring *The Invisible Gorilla*

Cass Sunstein (b. 1954) is a Harvard-based lecturer in law and behavioral economics who has co-authored books with Richard Thaler. Between the years of 2009 and 2014 he was America's most cited legal scholar.

Nassim Nicholas Taleb (b. 1960) is a Lebanese scholar who is currently Distinguished Professor of Risk Engineering at New York University. He wrote the extremely influential 2008 book *The Black Swan*, about how markets respond to highly improbable events.

Richard Thaler (b. 1945) is often cited by Kahneman and Tversky as a founding father of behavioral economics. He is a long-time collaborator of Kahneman and currently the Ralph and Dorothy Keller Distinguished Service Professor of Behavioral Science and Economics at the University of Chicago Booth School of Business.

Donald Trump (b. 1946) is the current and 45th President of the United States.

Amos Tversky (1937–96) was a long-time collaborator and "academic soul mate" of Daniel Kahneman. They worked on prospect theory and judgment under uncertainty together, for which Kahneman was later awarded the Nobel Prize.

WORKS CITED

WORKS CITED

Adams, Tim "Nudge Economics: Has push come to shove for a fashionable theory?" *The Guardian* June 1, 2014. Accessed October 19, 2017. https://www.theguardian.com/science/2014/jun/01/nudge-economics-freakonomics-daniel-kahneman-debunked

Ariely, Dan. *Predictably Irrational*. New York: HarperCollins, 2008.

Ariely, Dan and Simon Jones. *The (Honest) Truth about Dishonesty: How We Lie to Everyone, Especially Ourselves*. New York: HarperCollins, 2012.

The Upside of Irrationality. New York: HarperCollins, 2010.

Asch, Solomon E. and H. Guetzkow. "Effects of group pressure upon the modification and distortion of judgments." *Groups, Leadership, and Men* (1951): 222-236.

Bargh, John. A. "Priming Effects Replicate Just Fine, Thanks" *Psychology Today,* May 11, 2012. Retrieved October 20, 2017. https://www.psychologytoday.com/blog/the-natural-unconscious/201205/priming-effects-replicate-just-fine-thanks.

Becker, Gary. *The Economic Approach to Human Behavior*. Chicago: University of Chicago Press, 2013.

The Charlie Rose Show: https://charlierose.com/videos/15620. Accessed September 12, 2017

Debiec, Jacek. "Neuroscience: Capturing free will." *Nature* 478, no. 7369 (2011): 322-323.

Doyen, Stephanie, Olivier Klein, Cora-Lise Pichon, and Axel Cleeremans. "Behavioral priming: it's all in the mind, but whose mind?." *Plosone* 7:1 (2012).

Easterly, William. "Thinking, Fast and Slow." *The Financial Times* November 5, 2011. Retrieved September 13, 2017. https://www.ft.com/content/15bb6522-04ac-11e1-91d9-00144feabdc0.

The Economist. "Not so Smart Now" October 9, 2011. Retrieved September 12, 2017. http://www.economist.com/node/21534752.

Freakonomics Radio: http://freakonomics.com/2011/11/28/daniel-kahneman-answers-your-questions/. Accessed September 12, 2017.

Gladwell, Malcolm. *Blink: The Power of Thinking without Thinking*. Boston: Back Bay Books, 2007.

The Guardian, "Daniel Kahneman Changed the Way We Think About Thinking. But What Do Other Thinkers Think of Him," February 16, 2014. Accessed September 14, 2017. https://www.theguardian.com/science/2014/feb/16/daniel-kahneman-thinking-fast-and-slow-tributes.

Jones, Malcolm, and Lucas Wittman. "Fall Books Preview: From Murakami to Joan Didion." *The Daily Beast* February 9, 2011. Accessed August 21, 2017. http://www.thedailybeast.com/fall-books-preview-from-murakami-to-joan-didion.

Kahneman, Daniel. *Attention and Effort*. Englewood Cliffs, NJ: Prentice-Hall, 1973.

"Biographical," *Nobelprize.org*. Accessed August 21, 2016, https://www.nobelprize.org/nobel_prizes/economic-sciences/laureates/2002/kahneman-bio.html.

Kahneman, Daniel, and Gary Klein. "Conditions for intuitive expertise: a failure to disagree." *American Psychologist* 64:6 (2009): 515-526.

Kahneman, Daniel, and Amos Tversky. "Prospect theory: An analysis of decision under risk." *Econometrica: Journal of the Econometric Society* (1979): 263-291. Levine, David K. *Is Behavioral Economics Doomed? The Ordinary Versus the Extraordinary*. Cambridge, UK: Open Book Publishers, 2012.

Levitt, Steven D., and Stephen J. Dubner. *Freakonomics: a rogue economist explores the hidden side of everything*. New York: William Morrow, 2005.

Lewis, Michael. *The Big Short: Inside the Doomsday Machine*. London, Penguin 2011.

The Undoing Project: A Friendship that Changed the World. London: Penguin, 2016.

Lewis, Michael, interviewed by Stephen Dubner. "The Men who Started a Thinking Revolution." http://freakonomics.com/podcast/men-started-thinking-revolution/. Accessed August 21, 2017Lowenstein, Roger. "Book Review: Thinking, Fast and Slow by Daniel Kahneman." *Bloomberg* October 28, 2011. Accessed August 22, 2017. https://www.bloomberg.com/news/articles/2011-10-27/book-review-thinking-fast-and-slow-by-daniel-kahneman.

Meehl. Paul E. *Clinical Versus Statistical Prediction: A Theoretical Analysis and a Review of the Evidence*. Minneapolis: University of Minnesota Press, 1954.

Milgram, Stanley. "Behavioral Study of obedience." *The Journal of Abnormal and Social Psychology* 67, no. 4 (1963): 371-8.

Obedience to Authority: An Experimental View. NY: Harper Collins, 1974.Pinker, Steven. *The Better Angels of Our Nature: The Decline of Violence in History and its Causes*. London: Penguin, 2011.

Popova, Maria. "The Anti-Gladwell: Kahneman's New Way to Think About Thinking." *The Atlantic* November 1, 2011. Accessed September 6, 2017. https://www.theatlantic.com/health/archive/2011/11/the-anti-gladwell-kahnemans-new-way-to-think-about-thinking/247407/.

Shariatmadari, David. "Daniel Kahneman: 'What would I eliminate if I had a magic wand? Overconfidence'" *The Guardian* July 18, 2015.

Simon, Herbert. "A Behavioral Model of Rational Choice", in *Models of Man, Social and Rational: Mathematical Essays on Rational Human Behavior in a Social Setting*. New York: Wiley, 1957.

Taleb, Nassim Nicholas *The Black Swan: The Impact of the Highly Improbable*. NY: Random House, 2007.

Thaler, Richard, and Cass Sunstein. *Nudge: The Gentle Power of Choice Architecture*. New Haven: Yale, 2008.

Tversky, Amos, and Daniel Kahneman. "Belief in the law of small numbers." *Psychological Bulletin* 76:2 (1971): 105.Tversky, Amos, and Daniel Kahneman. "Judgment under uncertainty: Heuristics and biases." In *Utility, probability, and human decision-making*, eds. Dirk Wendt and C.A. Vlek. Netherlands: Springer, 1975.

THE MACAT LIBRARY
BY DISCIPLINE

AFRICANA STUDIES

Chinua Achebe's *An Image of Africa: Racism in Conrad's Heart of Darkness*
W. E. B. Du Bois's *The Souls of Black Folk*
Zora Neale Huston's *Characteristics of Negro Expression*
Martin Luther King Jr's *Why We Can't Wait*
Toni Morrison's *Playing in the Dark: Whiteness in the American Literary Imagination*

ANTHROPOLOGY

Arjun Appadurai's *Modernity at Large: Cultural Dimensions of Globalisation*
Philippe Ariès's *Centuries of Childhood*
Franz Boas's *Race, Language and Culture*
Kim Chan & Renée Mauborgne's *Blue Ocean Strategy*
Jared Diamond's *Guns, Germs & Steel: the Fate of Human Societies*
Jared Diamond's *Collapse: How Societies Choose to Fail or Survive*
E. E. Evans-Pritchard's *Witchcraft, Oracles and Magic Among the Azande*
James Ferguson's *The Anti-Politics Machine*
Clifford Geertz's *The Interpretation of Cultures*
David Graeber's *Debt: the First 5000 Years*
Karen Ho's *Liquidated: An Ethnography of Wall Street*
Geert Hofstede's *Culture's Consequences: Comparing Values, Behaviors, Institutes and Organizations across Nations*
Claude Lévi-Strauss's *Structural Anthropology*
Jay Macleod's *Ain't No Makin' It: Aspirations and Attainment in a Low-Income Neighborhood*
Saba Mahmood's *The Politics of Piety: The Islamic Revival and the Feminist Subject*
Marcel Mauss's *The Gift*

BUSINESS

Jean Lave & Etienne Wenger's *Situated Learning*
Theodore Levitt's *Marketing Myopia*
Burton G. Malkiel's *A Random Walk Down Wall Street*
Douglas McGregor's *The Human Side of Enterprise*
Michael Porter's *Competitive Strategy: Creating and Sustaining Superior Performance*
John Kotter's *Leading Change*
C. K. Prahalad & Gary Hamel's *The Core Competence of the Corporation*

CRIMINOLOGY

Michelle Alexander's *The New Jim Crow: Mass Incarceration in the Age of Colorblindness*
Michael R. Gottfredson & Travis Hirschi's *A General Theory of Crime*
Richard Herrnstein & Charles A. Murray's *The Bell Curve: Intelligence and Class Structure in American Life*
Elizabeth Loftus's *Eyewitness Testimony*
Jay Macleod's *Ain't No Makin' It: Aspirations and Attainment in a Low-Income Neighborhood*
Philip Zimbardo's *The Lucifer Effect*

ECONOMICS

Janet Abu-Lughod's *Before European Hegemony*
Ha-Joon Chang's *Kicking Away the Ladder*
David Brion Davis's *The Problem of Slavery in the Age of Revolution*
Milton Friedman's *The Role of Monetary Policy*
Milton Friedman's *Capitalism and Freedom*
David Graeber's *Debt: the First 5000 Years*
Friedrich Hayek's *The Road to Serfdom*
Karen Ho's *Liquidated: An Ethnography of Wall Street*

The Macat Library By Discipline

John Maynard Keynes's *The General Theory of Employment, Interest and Money*
Charles P. Kindleberger's *Manias, Panics and Crashes*
Robert Lucas's *Why Doesn't Capital Flow from Rich to Poor Countries?*
Burton G. Malkiel's *A Random Walk Down Wall Street*
Thomas Robert Malthus's *An Essay on the Principle of Population*
Karl Marx's *Capital*
Thomas Piketty's *Capital in the Twenty-First Century*
Amartya Sen's *Development as Freedom*
Adam Smith's *The Wealth of Nations*
Nassim Nicholas Taleb's *The Black Swan: The Impact of the Highly Improbable*
Amos Tversky's & Daniel Kahneman's *Judgment under Uncertainty: Heuristics and Biases*
Mahbub Ul Haq's *Reflections on Human Development*
Max Weber's *The Protestant Ethic and the Spirit of Capitalism*

FEMINISM AND GENDER STUDIES

Judith Butler's *Gender Trouble*
Simone De Beauvoir's *The Second Sex*
Michel Foucault's *History of Sexuality*
Betty Friedan's *The Feminine Mystique*
Saba Mahmood's *The Politics of Piety: The Islamic Revival and the Feminist Subject*
Joan Wallach Scott's *Gender and the Politics of History*
Mary Wollstonecraft's *A Vindication of the Rights of Woman*
Virginia Woolf's *A Room of One's Own*

GEOGRAPHY

The Brundtland Report's *Our Common Future*
Rachel Carson's *Silent Spring*
Charles Darwin's *On the Origin of Species*
James Ferguson's *The Anti-Politics Machine*
Jane Jacobs's *The Death and Life of Great American Cities*
James Lovelock's *Gaia: A New Look at Life on Earth*
Amartya Sen's *Development as Freedom*
Mathis Wackernagel & William Rees's *Our Ecological Footprint*

HISTORY

Janet Abu-Lughod's *Before European Hegemony*
Benedict Anderson's *Imagined Communities*
Bernard Bailyn's *The Ideological Origins of the American Revolution*
Hanna Batatu's *The Old Social Classes And The Revolutionary Movements Of Iraq*
Christopher Browning's *Ordinary Men: Reserve Police Batallion 101 and the Final Solution in Poland*
Edmund Burke's *Reflections on the Revolution in France*
William Cronon's *Nature's Metropolis: Chicago And The Great West*
Alfred W. Crosby's *The Columbian Exchange*
Hamid Dabashi's *Iran: A People Interrupted*
David Brion Davis's *The Problem of Slavery in the Age of Revolution*
Nathalie Zemon Davis's *The Return of Martin Guerre*
Jared Diamond's *Guns, Germs & Steel: the Fate of Human Societies*
Frank Dikotter's *Mao's Great Famine*
John W Dower's *War Without Mercy: Race And Power In The Pacific War*
W. E. B. Du Bois's *The Souls of Black Folk*
Richard J. Evans's *In Defence of History*
Lucien Febvre's *The Problem of Unbelief in the 16th Century*
Sheila Fitzpatrick's *Everyday Stalinism*

Eric Foner's *Reconstruction: America's Unfinished Revolution, 1863-1877*
Michel Foucault's *Discipline and Punish*
Michel Foucault's *History of Sexuality*
Francis Fukuyama's *The End of History and the Last Man*
John Lewis Gaddis's *We Now Know: Rethinking Cold War History*
Ernest Gellner's *Nations and Nationalism*
Eugene Genovese's *Roll, Jordan, Roll: The World the Slaves Made*
Carlo Ginzburg's *The Night Battles*
Daniel Goldhagen's *Hitler's Willing Executioners*
Jack Goldstone's *Revolution and Rebellion in the Early Modern World*
Antonio Gramsci's *The Prison Notebooks*
Alexander Hamilton, John Jay & James Madison's *The Federalist Papers*
Christopher Hill's *The World Turned Upside Down*
Carole Hillenbrand's *The Crusades: Islamic Perspectives*
Thomas Hobbes's *Leviathan*
Eric Hobsbawm's *The Age Of Revolution*
John A. Hobson's *Imperialism: A Study*
Albert Hourani's *History of the Arab Peoples*
Samuel P. Huntington's *The Clash of Civilizations and the Remaking of World Order*
C. L. R. James's *The Black Jacobins*
Tony Judt's *Postwar: A History of Europe Since 1945*
Ernst Kantorowicz's *The King's Two Bodies: A Study in Medieval Political Theology*
Paul Kennedy's *The Rise and Fall of the Great Powers*
Ian Kershaw's *The "Hitler Myth": Image and Reality in the Third Reich*
John Maynard Keynes's *The General Theory of Employment, Interest and Money*
Charles P. Kindleberger's *Manias, Panics and Crashes*
Martin Luther King Jr's *Why We Can't Wait*
Henry Kissinger's *World Order: Reflections on the Character of Nations and the Course of History*
Thomas Kuhn's *The Structure of Scientific Revolutions*
Georges Lefebvre's *The Coming of the French Revolution*
John Locke's *Two Treatises of Government*
Niccolò Machiavelli's *The Prince*
Thomas Robert Malthus's *An Essay on the Principle of Population*
Mahmood Mamdani's *Citizen and Subject: Contemporary Africa And The Legacy Of Late Colonialism*
Karl Marx's *Capital*
Stanley Milgram's *Obedience to Authority*
John Stuart Mill's *On Liberty*
Thomas Paine's *Common Sense*
Thomas Paine's *Rights of Man*
Geoffrey Parker's *Global Crisis: War, Climate Change and Catastrophe in the Seventeenth Century*
Jonathan Riley-Smith's *The First Crusade and the Idea of Crusading*
Jean-Jacques Rousseau's *The Social Contract*
Joan Wallach Scott's *Gender and the Politics of History*
Theda Skocpol's *States and Social Revolutions*
Adam Smith's *The Wealth of Nations*
Timothy Snyder's *Bloodlands: Europe Between Hitler and Stalin*
Sun Tzu's *The Art of War*
Keith Thomas's *Religion and the Decline of Magic*
Thucydides's *The History of the Peloponnesian War*
Frederick Jackson Turner's *The Significance of the Frontier in American History*
Odd Arne Westad's *The Global Cold War: Third World Interventions And The Making Of Our Times*

LITERATURE

Chinua Achebe's *An Image of Africa: Racism in Conrad's Heart of Darkness*
Roland Barthes's *Mythologies*
Homi K. Bhabha's *The Location of Culture*
Judith Butler's *Gender Trouble*
Simone De Beauvoir's *The Second Sex*
Ferdinand De Saussure's *Course in General Linguistics*
T. S. Eliot's *The Sacred Wood: Essays on Poetry and Criticism*
Zora Neale Huston's *Characteristics of Negro Expression*
Toni Morrison's *Playing in the Dark: Whiteness in the American Literary Imagination*
Edward Said's *Orientalism*
Gayatri Chakravorty Spivak's *Can the Subaltern Speak?*
Mary Wollstonecraft's *A Vindication of the Rights of Women*
Virginia Woolf's *A Room of One's Own*

PHILOSOPHY

Elizabeth Anscombe's *Modern Moral Philosophy*
Hannah Arendt's *The Human Condition*
Aristotle's *Metaphysics*
Aristotle's *Nicomachean Ethics*
Edmund Gettier's *Is Justified True Belief Knowledge?*
Georg Wilhelm Friedrich Hegel's *Phenomenology of Spirit*
David Hume's *Dialogues Concerning Natural Religion*
David Hume's *The Enquiry for Human Understanding*
Immanuel Kant's *Religion within the Boundaries of Mere Reason*
Immanuel Kant's *Critique of Pure Reason*
Søren Kierkegaard's *The Sickness Unto Death*
Søren Kierkegaard's *Fear and Trembling*
C. S. Lewis's *The Abolition of Man*
Alasdair MacIntyre's *After Virtue*
Marcus Aurelius's *Meditations*
Friedrich Nietzsche's *On the Genealogy of Morality*
Friedrich Nietzsche's *Beyond Good and Evil*
Plato's *Republic*
Plato's *Symposium*
Jean-Jacques Rousseau's *The Social Contract*
Gilbert Ryle's *The Concept of Mind*
Baruch Spinoza's *Ethics*
Sun Tzu's *The Art of War*
Ludwig Wittgenstein's *Philosophical Investigations*

POLITICS

Benedict Anderson's *Imagined Communities*
Aristotle's *Politics*
Bernard Bailyn's *The Ideological Origins of the American Revolution*
Edmund Burke's *Reflections on the Revolution in France*
John C. Calhoun's *A Disquisition on Government*
Ha-Joon Chang's *Kicking Away the Ladder*
Hamid Dabashi's *Iran: A People Interrupted*
Hamid Dabashi's *Theology of Discontent: The Ideological Foundation of the Islamic Revolution in Iran*
Robert Dahl's *Democracy and its Critics*
Robert Dahl's *Who Governs?*
David Brion Davis's *The Problem of Slavery in the Age of Revolution*

Alexis De Tocqueville's *Democracy in America*
James Ferguson's *The Anti-Politics Machine*
Frank Dikotter's *Mao's Great Famine*
Sheila Fitzpatrick's *Everyday Stalinism*
Eric Foner's *Reconstruction: America's Unfinished Revolution, 1863-1877*
Milton Friedman's *Capitalism and Freedom*
Francis Fukuyama's *The End of History and the Last Man*
John Lewis Gaddis's *We Now Know: Rethinking Cold War History*
Ernest Gellner's *Nations and Nationalism*
David Graeber's *Debt: the First 5000 Years*
Antonio Gramsci's *The Prison Notebooks*
Alexander Hamilton, John Jay & James Madison's *The Federalist Papers*
Friedrich Hayek's *The Road to Serfdom*
Christopher Hill's *The World Turned Upside Down*
Thomas Hobbes's *Leviathan*
John A. Hobson's *Imperialism: A Study*
Samuel P. Huntington's *The Clash of Civilizations and the Remaking of World Order*
Tony Judt's *Postwar: A History of Europe Since 1945*
David C. Kang's *China Rising: Peace, Power and Order in East Asia*
Paul Kennedy's *The Rise and Fall of Great Powers*
Robert Keohane's *After Hegemony*
Martin Luther King Jr.'s *Why We Can't Wait*
Henry Kissinger's *World Order: Reflections on the Character of Nations and the Course of History*
John Locke's *Two Treatises of Government*
Niccolò Machiavelli's *The Prince*
Thomas Robert Malthus's *An Essay on the Principle of Population*
Mahmood Mamdani's *Citizen and Subject: Contemporary Africa And The Legacy Of Late Colonialism*
Karl Marx's *Capital*
John Stuart Mill's *On Liberty*
John Stuart Mill's *Utilitarianism*
Hans Morgenthau's *Politics Among Nations*
Thomas Paine's *Common Sense*
Thomas Paine's *Rights of Man*
Thomas Piketty's *Capital in the Twenty-First Century*
Robert D. Putman's *Bowling Alone*
John Rawls's *Theory of Justice*
Jean-Jacques Rousseau's *The Social Contract*
Theda Skocpol's *States and Social Revolutions*
Adam Smith's *The Wealth of Nations*
Sun Tzu's *The Art of War*
Henry David Thoreau's *Civil Disobedience*
Thucydides's *The History of the Peloponnesian War*
Kenneth Waltz's *Theory of International Politics*
Max Weber's *Politics as a Vocation*
Odd Arne Westad's *The Global Cold War: Third World Interventions And The Making Of Our Times*

POSTCOLONIAL STUDIES

Roland Barthes's *Mythologies*
Frantz Fanon's *Black Skin, White Masks*
Homi K. Bhabha's *The Location of Culture*
Gustavo Gutiérrez's *A Theology of Liberation*
Edward Said's *Orientalism*
Gayatri Chakravorty Spivak's *Can the Subaltern Speak?*

The Macat Library By Discipline

PSYCHOLOGY

Gordon Allport's *The Nature of Prejudice*
Alan Baddeley & Graham Hitch's *Aggression: A Social Learning Analysis*
Albert Bandura's *Aggression: A Social Learning Analysis*
Leon Festinger's *A Theory of Cognitive Dissonance*
Sigmund Freud's *The Interpretation of Dreams*
Betty Friedan's *The Feminine Mystique*
Michael R. Gottfredson & Travis Hirschi's *A General Theory of Crime*
Eric Hoffer's *The True Believer: Thoughts on the Nature of Mass Movements*
William James's *Principles of Psychology*
Elizabeth Loftus's *Eyewitness Testimony*
A. H. Maslow's *A Theory of Human Motivation*
Stanley Milgram's *Obedience to Authority*
Steven Pinker's *The Better Angels of Our Nature*
Oliver Sacks's *The Man Who Mistook His Wife For a Hat*
Richard Thaler & Cass Sunstein's *Nudge: Improving Decisions About Health, Wealth and Happiness*
Amos Tversky's *Judgment under Uncertainty: Heuristics and Biases*
Philip Zimbardo's *The Lucifer Effect*

SCIENCE

Rachel Carson's *Silent Spring*
William Cronon's *Nature's Metropolis: Chicago And The Great West*
Alfred W. Crosby's *The Columbian Exchange*
Charles Darwin's *On the Origin of Species*
Richard Dawkin's *The Selfish Gene*
Thomas Kuhn's *The Structure of Scientific Revolutions*
Geoffrey Parker's *Global Crisis: War, Climate Change and Catastrophe in the Seventeenth Century*
Mathis Wackernagel & William Rees's *Our Ecological Footprint*

SOCIOLOGY

Michelle Alexander's *The New Jim Crow: Mass Incarceration in the Age of Colorblindness*
Gordon Allport's *The Nature of Prejudice*
Albert Bandura's *Aggression: A Social Learning Analysis*
Hanna Batatu's *The Old Social Classes And The Revolutionary Movements Of Iraq*
Ha-Joon Chang's *Kicking Away the Ladder*
W. E. B. Du Bois's *The Souls of Black Folk*
Émile Durkheim's *On Suicide*
Frantz Fanon's *Black Skin, White Masks*
Frantz Fanon's *The Wretched of the Earth*
Eric Foner's *Reconstruction: America's Unfinished Revolution, 1863-1877*
Eugene Genovese's *Roll, Jordan, Roll: The World the Slaves Made*
Jack Goldstone's *Revolution and Rebellion in the Early Modern World*
Antonio Gramsci's *The Prison Notebooks*
Richard Herrnstein & Charles A Murray's *The Bell Curve: Intelligence and Class Structure in American Life*
Eric Hoffer's *The True Believer: Thoughts on the Nature of Mass Movements*
Jane Jacobs's *The Death and Life of Great American Cities*
Robert Lucas's *Why Doesn't Capital Flow from Rich to Poor Countries?*
Jay Macleod's *Ain't No Makin' It: Aspirations and Attainment in a Low Income Neighborhood*
Elaine May's *Homeward Bound: American Families in the Cold War Era*
Douglas McGregor's *The Human Side of Enterprise*
C. Wright Mills's *The Sociological Imagination*

Thomas Piketty's *Capital in the Twenty-First Century*
Robert D. Putman's *Bowling Alone*
David Riesman's *The Lonely Crowd: A Study of the Changing American Character*
Edward Said's *Orientalism*
Joan Wallach Scott's *Gender and the Politics of History*
Theda Skocpol's *States and Social Revolutions*
Max Weber's *The Protestant Ethic and the Spirit of Capitalism*

THEOLOGY

Augustine's *Confessions*
Benedict's *Rule of St Benedict*
Gustavo Gutiérrez's *A Theology of Liberation*
Carole Hillenbrand's *The Crusades: Islamic Perspectives*
David Hume's *Dialogues Concerning Natural Religion*
Immanuel Kant's *Religion within the Boundaries of Mere Reason*
Ernst Kantorowicz's *The King's Two Bodies: A Study in Medieval Political Theology*
Søren Kierkegaard's *The Sickness Unto Death*
C. S. Lewis's *The Abolition of Man*
Saba Mahmood's *The Politics of Piety: The Islamic Revival and the Feminist Subject*
Baruch Spinoza's *Ethics*
Keith Thomas's *Religion and the Decline of Magic*

COMING SOON

Chris Argyris's *The Individual and the Organisation*
Seyla Benhabib's *The Rights of Others*
Walter Benjamin's *The Work Of Art in the Age of Mechanical Reproduction*
John Berger's *Ways of Seeing*
Pierre Bourdieu's *Outline of a Theory of Practice*
Mary Douglas's *Purity and Danger*
Roland Dworkin's *Taking Rights Seriously*
James G. March's *Exploration and Exploitation in Organisational Learning*
Ikujiro Nonaka's *A Dynamic Theory of Organizational Knowledge Creation*
Griselda Pollock's *Vision and Difference*
Amartya Sen's *Inequality Re-Examined*
Susan Sontag's *On Photography*
Yasser Tabbaa's *The Transformation of Islamic Art*
Ludwig von Mises's *Theory of Money and Credit*

Macat Disciplines

Access the greatest ideas and thinkers across entire disciplines, including

Postcolonial Studies

Roland Barthes's *Mythologies*
Frantz Fanon's *Black Skin, White Masks*
Homi K. Bhabha's *The Location of Culture*
Gustavo Gutiérrez's *A Theology of Liberation*
Edward Said's *Orientalism*
Gayatri Chakravorty Spivak's *Can the Subaltern Speak?*

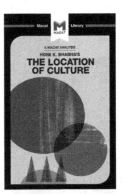

Macat Disciplines

Access the greatest ideas and thinkers across entire disciplines, including

AFRICANA STUDIES

Chinua Achebe's *An Image of Africa: Racism in Conrad's Heart of Darkness*

W. E. B. Du Bois's *The Souls of Black Folk*

Zora Neale Hurston's *Characteristics of Negro Expression*

Martin Luther King Jr.'s *Why We Can't Wait*

Toni Morrison's *Playing in the Dark: Whiteness in the American Literary Imagination*

Macat analyses are available from all good bookshops and libraries.

Access hundreds of analyses through one, multimedia tool.
Join free for one month **library.macat.com**

Macat Disciplines

Access the greatest ideas and thinkers across entire disciplines, including

FEMINISM, GENDER AND QUEER STUDIES

Simone De Beauvoir's
The Second Sex

Michel Foucault's
History of Sexuality

Betty Friedan's
The Feminine Mystique

Saba Mahmood's
*The Politics of Piety:
The Islamic Revival and
the Feminist Subject*

Joan Wallach Scott's
*Gender and the
Politics of History*

Mary Wollstonecraft's
*A Vindication of the
Rights of Woman*

Virginia Woolf's
A Room of One's Own

Judith Butler's
Gender Trouble

Macat analyses are available from all good bookshops and libraries.

Access hundreds of analyses through one, multimedia tool.
Join free for one month **library.macat.com**